Encouraging
In Young Children

A guidebook for parents

by Dr. Don Weinhouse

Illustrated by Deborah Zemke

BARRON'S

All inquiries should be addressed to:
Barron's Educational Series, Inc.
250 Wireless Boulevard
Hauppauge, New York 11788

Library of Congress Catalog Card No. 97-15976
International Standard Book No. 0-7641-0252-4

Library of Congress Cataloging-in-Publication Data
Weinhouse, Don, 1947–
    Encouraging potential in young children : a guidebook for parents
/ Don Weinhouse.
        p. cm.
    Includes bibliographical references and index.
    ISBN 0-7641-0252-4
    1. Child rearing. 2. Child development 3. Parent and child.
    I. Title.
HQ772.W3615 1998
649'.1—dc21   97-15976
                                                   CIP

Printed in the United States of America
9 8 7 6 5 4 3 2

TABLE OF CONTENTS

DEDICATION

This book is dedicated to my mother and father, Shirley and Jerry Weinhouse, and the many other parents whom I have observed enriching their children's lives through the powerful techniques described in this book. To:

Michael and Helena Atlas-Acuna
Mary Bailey
Sherwyn and Marilyn Bulmash
Jim and Kyle Christian
Rocky Deniro
Wilma and Howard Friedman
Nancy and Peter Fishman
Frank and Sue Grijalva
Julie Gordon
Barbara Handel
Jill Holmes
Joyce Huggins
Richard and Ava Jay
Paul and Barb Kelter
Norm and Linda Levitt
Brent, Julie, Gary, and Ellen Morse
Gordon and Marsha Nelson
Connie Nash
Velda Spicer
Roger, Fred, and Claudia Weinhouse
Al and Helene Ziman

And my own wife Marilyn, who, through her patience, love, attention, and devotion to our daughter Rachel, has taught me the most—I thank you.

PREFACE

What's a parent to do? On the one hand, television, magazines, and books are providing us with all sorts of programs and techniques that are supposed to supercharge our children's intelligence, achievement, and overall development, lead them to appropriate and civilized behavior, and create in them a strong and positive sense of self and psychological-social health. On the other hand, we're being warned about pushing too hard or too fast, stealing away their childhood, and the million and one mistakes we can make that might lead them to lives of neurotic, disempowered, codependent, egocentric, overeating, anorexic, gang-involved, drug-and-alcohol-dependent emptiness. What's a parent to do?

Well, the answer is simple: *we do our best!* And part of doing our best is reading books like this, books that clearly and concisely explain practical, everyday, tried-and-true, state-of-the-art approaches to working with our children. We read. We watch and talk to people who seem to be doing it well—this, by the way, is where most of the ideas in this book came from, from observing and talking to parents who are experiencing success encouraging their children's potential. We analyze the results of what we're doing and adjust accordingly.

You are invited to take and use what you like from these pages, and discard that which doesn't fit your system or style. All of the ideas in this book are compatible, but you do not need to use them all for any one idea to work; another unique feature of this book is that every page, every section, can stand on its own. There isn't a sequential order that you have to follow for these ideas to work, and you don't have to use the ideas in combination with one another. While an attempt was made to order the various parts into a sequential whole, the sections can be read and reread in any order.

The two keys or themes that run throughout the following pages are both mentioned in the title, and explained, reexplained, examined, and analyzed in many different sections. These are *encouragement* and *potential.*

- *Encouragement.* This book will teach you this useful and dynamic approach that motivates children to become involved in productive activities, and to learn, grow, and achieve—an approach that sets children up for success, helps them feel good about themselves and their accomplishments, makes them more responsible for their behaviors, and offers them the opportunity to investigate and learn more about who they are and where they're going.

- *Potential.* This book will lead you to more clearly identify, understand, and nurture your children's strengths / abilities / areas of potential. It will help you see possibilities you may never have seen before.

What you will probably enjoy most about this book is the way it merges theory and practice. Each section makes clear and concise recommendations, supported by both logic and experience. The ideas come from everyday practices of parents skillfully doing what is right for their children. As you read through the sections of this book, you will hopefully envision yourself and your children in each situation. So start at the beginning or start at the end (I'd recommend the beginning), and consider and experience all of the ideas and recommendations.

CHAPTER 1

WHAT IS POTENTIAL?

INTRODUCTION

Considering that *potential* is a key word in the title of this book, it seems appropriate that the term be explained prior to investigating how to encourage its development. Potential in the context of this book is the ceiling, the limit, the extreme, the very best your children have in them in each and every skill, ability, trait, and characteristic they possess. This ceiling is determined by a combination of biological inheritance (chromosomes and genes, sometimes called "nature"), the environment in which they are raised (their upbringing, sometimes called "nurture"), and personal motivation, the drive or desire to achieve or become (this motivation factor may well be a product of the combination of inheritance and environment, but it is of such importance that we will discuss it separately). Some writers, theologians, and theorists add other ingredients into the formula of potential—God, luck, astrology, karma—but, for the purposes of this chapter, we'll focus on *inheritance, environment,* and *motivation.*

Please keep in mind that maximizing potential isn't the same as being or becoming gifted or a genius. This group of individuals will receive special attention in Chapter 11 (Groups at Risk of Not Realizing Their Potential). No, maximizing potential doesn't mean being gifted or being a genius, it means doing the most with what you've got. This book and this chapter are written to guide parents—all parents—to help their children be the most they can be. Almost all of us have more in us (potential) than we are putting to use. The mission here is to help us activate what is in our children, but this doesn't mean that we are going to turn them into kids who are gifted or geniuses.

THE RELEVANCE OF POTENTIAL IN THE CONTEXT OF THIS BOOK

In order to help our children make the most they can of their lives, we must learn about and understand and help our children learn about and understand themselves. This knowledge can help us design experiences that will lead them to use their potential. The self-knowledge and understanding they gain may become powerful tools that can help them find meaning and direction in life and make important choices.

Through identifying areas of personal potential, parents and children have more data to help make decisions on hobbies to pursue, subjects to study, and future plans or goals.

We are unique meldings of our biological mothers' and fathers' genetic makeup, and it is their union, the combination of their genes, that determines many of our physical, intellectual, psychological, and social traits. In the area of potential, our inheritance determines what might be considered the outer limits of who and what we may become—the best or most that lies within us. Given these guidelines, it is then the job of environment/life experiences and our own degree of motivation or drive to help us reach these unseen potentials. For purposes of clarity, let's take a focused, detailed look at each of the separate ingredients in the potential formula.

• •

inheritance/genetics/nature
environment/upbringing/nurture
motivation/drive/desire

• •

INHERITANCE

D epending on the specific characteristic, the power of inheritance can range from complete and profound (as in eye color, blood type, and basic facial features), to moderate (as in physical coordination, temperament, and intelligence), to mild or perhaps even nonexistent (as in food preferences, accent, and preferred television shows). Here are examples to illustrate these factors.

In the absence of severe malnutrition or a significant overdose of hormone pills or shots, Sallie, age one day old, will someday be between 5 feet 2 inches and 5 feet 4 inches in height. Her potential is 5 feet 4 inches.

Mike, age birth-minus-two-months, will have brown hair. It may be light brown, or dark brown, depending on how much sun he gets; but, unless he bleaches it, his hair will be brown. His natural, unbleached potential is brown hair.

Abby, a six-month-old, was born with a supercharged brain (a nontechnical, but very descriptive term). Her family tree is filled with highly gifted scientists and mathematicians, who have or had extremely high abilities and achievement levels in certain areas. If Abby receives a typical upbringing, and avoids brain-damaging accidents, her genetic makeup has predetermined that she has tremendous potential (gifted to highly gifted /genius range) in mathematic and scientific intelligence. Her potential is highly gifted in math and science.

Abby's brother, who is two years old and born of the same parents, will almost certainly never be a brilliant scientist or mathematician. His genetic makeup has provided him with a brain that will probably be somewhere around average in science and math. He may have a choice of many wonderful careers, but a brilliant mathematician or scientist he will not be, and he will always need to put much more time and effort than his younger sister into learning in these areas. His potential is slightly above average in math and science.

* *

Carol is only 18 months old, but already has begun to demonstrate excellent physical coordination. While there is no way to measure her exact potential, all who see her agree that she has a special gift in using her body efficiently. There are no great, or even good athletes or dancers in her family background, so her parents are a bit puzzled as to how and why, at her very young age, she can walk and run so well, do a forward roll, and is starting to learn to catch, throw, kick, and bounce balls—skills that most children twice her age are only beginning to develop. The answer, once again, is inheritance. Somehow, the genetic formulas of her mother and father that merged to create little Carol combined themselves in such a way as to provide her with a neuromuscular system that is far more advanced than the average child of her age. Her potential is excellent in physical coordination and perhaps sports and/or dance.

* *

If brought up in a typical family environment, without special attention to her unique personality and psychological-social predispositions (inheritance), Jane, three years old, will emerge into adulthood as a neurotic and unhappy woman. She has been born with a very challenging psychological-social genetic make-up that, in order for her to maximize her innate potential, will require her parents, relatives, friends, and teachers to provide her with more attention, both personal and professional, than most children need. The potential for Jane to experience a joyous and fulfilling life exists; however, for her potential in this area to be actualized, a vast array of resources will need to be brought together.

* *

Julia was born with Down's syndrome, a genetic condition that usually leads to mental retardation and a number of unique physical characteristics. While some children with Down's syndrome enter adulthood severely retarded, most have only mild or moderate retardation, and some fall in the average IQ range.

In Julia's case, a highly stimulating life will lead her to an intelligence level in the low average/borderline range, or an IQ of 75–80. Julia's potential is low average/borderline intelligence.

Children are not their parents. They often resemble their parents in a variety of ways but they are not their parents. While heredity plays an important role in many human traits, in others it is far less important.

The old expression, *There's more there than meets the eye* is a truth that applies not only to glaciers and calories, but also to people, young and old. *There's more there than meets the eye* is a statement that applies to you and your children's innate, inborn, thank you Mom and Dad, I'll-never-know-how-much-is-there-until-I-push-myself traits, built into each of our system's potentials in painting, music, math, cooking, swimming, writing, sewing, caring, and loving, not to mention jumping, singing, crocheting, juggling, listening, remembering, and sculpting!

ENVIRONMENT

Environment, sometimes referred to as upbringing or nurturing, includes many different factors. Among the most important of these are the following, which frequently overlap one another:

- ■ nutrition and health
- ■ sensory stimulation (including the senses of taste, smell, touch, movement/balance, hearing, and seeing)
- ■ mental stimulation (including language and thought)
- ■ relationships with parents, siblings, relatives, and others
- ■ cultural experiences, awareness, and sensitivity

Any ingredient in children's lives that influences how they experience their existence or perceive themselves is a component of their environment.

Many types of researchers (medical, psychological, social, educational) are constantly studying the effects that changes in the environments children are brought up in have on who those children might become. While we are just scratching the surface of understanding in this area, much knowledge has been gathered. For example:

The quality of nutrition has an influence on children's physical growth; in cases of severe malnutrition individuals do not grow as large as their genetic potential might have allowed them to and with more physical and health needs than their genetic potential might have predicted.

Children who are abused (mentally, physically, or sexually) have a higher likelihood of someday becoming abusers than children who did not endure such unfortunate experiences.

Children brought up in cultures where people touch more and speak to one another from a closer distance tend to become adults who touch more and speak to one another from a closer distance.

Children raised in environments where violence is more often witnessed or physically experienced, as well as children who watch significant amounts of violence on television, become more hostile and violent; they tend to copy, or act out the behavior themselves.

Children raised in homes where there is minimal language stimulation, where few books are present, and materials and toys are not provided on a regular basis, develop lower levels of intelligence than similar children (those with approximately the same potential) who are provided with these advantages.

Time spent listening to and speaking a second language, during the first few years of children's lives most often yields greater levels of proficiency with much better pronunciation

> *than equivalent amounts of time trying to learn to understand and speak the same second language in later childhood or in adulthood.*

Our environments help mold who we are and how we behave. Children born into more enriching environments will, in general, have higher likelihoods of developing more areas of potential, or more fully actualizing themselves in more areas of their potential, than will children born into disadvantaged life situations. On the other hand, poverty and other significant environmental challenges (such as being raised in a country at war, growing up 200 miles from the closest town and neighbors, living in a home with an emotionally disturbed or mentally retarded parent) create situations that can be profoundly challenging to both children and adults. (Groups at risk of not maximizing their potential are discussed in Chapter 11.)

Our genetic inheritance sets the stage upon which our environments go to work. The environments in which children are raised can help lead them into more fully actualizing their potential but cannot move them beyond whatever their inborn potential is. The environments in which children are raised can also lead them away from the development of potential and force them to focus more on basic survival and perhaps into bad habits and less than desirable traits.

MOTIVATION

Over the past several years a number of theorists have pointed to motivation as a critical variable in the actualization of potential. Stated simply, the theory is as follows.

There are a lot of people with great genes (the genetic potential to be great scholars, athletes, leaders, artists, and so on) who have been provided with enriching environments (wonderful nutrition, caring and loving parents, great stimulation, good schools), but who never really put it all together and do very much with what they have. Some ingredient seems to be missing, and that ingredient is very often an intangible commodity that might be called motivation, or drive, or desire, or stick-to-itiveness, or task commitment.

Overachievers

The most obvious cases of motivation at work are those individuals, both children and adults, who are referred to as *overachievers* (a term that, once you finish reading this section, you will never again use). In truth, there is no such thing as an overachiever. Overachievers are individuals who, blessed with excellent motivation, are closer to realizing their potential than the rest of us. The sad truth of it is (not sad as in "let's get all depressed and start crying," but sad as in "it's time we do something to change this") that just about everyone, you and I included, is *underachieving*. The overachievers have more motivation, a better work ethic, than the rest of us; they use more of their potential than we do, so they are labeled overachievers.

Can you think of someone you know who you regard as an overachiever? Picture that person in your mind. What is it that they say or do that makes you think of them in this way? Now, ask yourself this question: Are they really overachieving— going beyond their potential—or, would it be more accurate to conceptualize them as very motivated people who just happen to be using more of their potential than most? I don't know what answer you just came up with, but when I meet someone who others regard as an overachiever I most often feel that I'm in the presence of a very special person who knows how to get the most out of what they've got. I rest my case! Wait, I can't rest yet. I must add one more critique of those who use the term overachiever. I accuse these people of libel. I accuse them of labeling what is truly a wonderful characteristic (motivation) with a negatively charged, derogatory, condescending term— overachiever.

To summarize the preceding tirade, it does get me a bit steamed up when I think about how we subtly put down individuals who are working hard by calling them negatively charged names (overachievers, type A, obsessive, one-sided, etc.). Most of us are underachievers, in that we don't use all our potential. In other words, overachievers are merely individuals who are less underachieving than the rest of us.

Now, have I convinced you to not use the term overachiever anymore? I hope so. The professor in me feels the need to quiz you, the reader, right now. Without looking back to the previous paragraphs, envision what is going to run through your mind the next time you hear a child or adult referred to as an overachiever.

THINK.

NOW CONTINUE WITH YOUR READING.

Underachievers

Most of us know or once knew people who were really good or great at something when they were younger. (The skills or abilities were probably visible at very young ages, which would indicate genetic potential.) They seemed to have been raised in an environment that nurtured or helped their development in this area but they never really did anything with their skill, or went as far as you and others thought they might have. What was missing? The ingredient that needed to be included to maximize these individuals' area of potential was probably motivation.

Let's take a look at some unnamed men and women who seemed to have it all (the genetic potential and a supportive environment) but, at the present time, don't seem to be maximizing their potentials (they are underachieving). Keep in mind that these cases are exaggerated, extreme, out of the ordinary. The idea to focus on here is that achievement is more than a simple formula of heredity + environment.

> *The tennis star blazed onto the courts at two years of age with incredible coordination, and supportive, loving, and dedicated parents. At twelve she was national juniors champion, won her high school state championship, went to college on a tennis scholarship, was the number one singles player during her freshman year, dropped off the team during her sophomore year and now, at 21, hasn't touched a tennis racket in two years.*

The handsome, friendly, verbally precocious three-year-old with the successful, loving, caring, socially aware, do-anything-for-our-child parents later starred in all the preschool and elementary school plays, was elected president of every club and every class, was nominated high school senior class best-looking, most social, and most likely to succeed, and now, at the age of 19, is not in school, doesn't have a job, and spends eight hours a day watching television.

The verbally precocious little boy, at five years of age, could read, write in sentences, add, subtract, multiply, and divide. His parents greatly prided themselves on his abilities and achievements, and did everything in their power to entice their little prodigy into the world of learning and knowledge. He did extremely well throughout school, but never went to college, and has spent the last few years bouncing from minimum wage job to minimum wage job.

Her parents were both archaeologists and, by the time she was 12 years old, she knew more about rocks, the formation of the earth, and the history of Homo sapiens than most college graduates with a B.A. in anthropology. Her parents deeply loved and cared for her, and took her on digs and exciting, adventurous vacations all over the world. By the age of 23 she had completed an M.A. in anthropology, published four articles, almost completed a book on the history of the Arkansas River Valley, and finished all course work and exams for her doctorate in cultural anthropology. She never finished her book or her doctorate, and today only occasionally reads on the topic. With little joy or self-fulfillment, she spends most of her waking hours cleaning house and cooking for her three young children, and complaining about how rough life is for a single mom who's 29 years old, overweight, on welfare, and has no plans or prospects for her future.

Shooting baskets, dribbling, playing defense..., this little boy was born to be a ball player. Not just "born to be," but raised by parents who loved basketball, played with him every day, took him to games, cherished his trophies, and often dreamed of his future as a star. High school coaches tried to "draft" him from his elementary school. Thirty colleges tried to convince this two-time high school "Player of the Year" to enter their schools. He entered a prestigious Big 10 basketball program on a full scholarship, only to drop out after three months, because he "didn't dig college." Now 20 years old, he still plays a little, when he's not busy hustling drugs on the street, or too stoned to walk a straight line.

The above individuals all had great potential and support-ive, nurturing environments, yet they were all people who fell short of their own and others' expectations. There are probably multiple reasons or causes for each of the scenarios just described; however, it is very probable that one of the major contributing factors in each case, *the,* or *one* of the missing ingredients relates to that intangible we're calling motivation, or drive, or desire, or stick-to-itiveness.

What about the opposite? There are individuals with less obvious potential and less nurturing environments, who manage to reach higher levels of achievement—what some people refer to as overachievers—but we know better! Consider the following.

She's the first black woman ever hired at this prestigious New York law firm. School records indicate only average performance in all subject areas from kindergarten through high school gradu-ation. IQ tests reveal above average ability, but not what might be considered intellectual giftedness. She was born into poverty, one of six children, and the first in her family to ever attend college. Despite having to work two jobs, a total of 50 hours a week over a period of six years, she earned her B.A. degree with highest honors and a full scholarship to Yale Law School, where she graduated in the top 10% of her class.

● ●

Quiet and shy throughout his school years, and never seeming to get very involved in anything, he was just another kid—just an average boy, growing up in an average town, in an average family. During his first few years selling clothes at a local department store, he continued his average status, not impress-ing his coworkers or supervisors with his abilities, potential, or motivation. Then it happened—over a period of eight short years he opened a small men's clothing store and developed it into a chain of six stores and a net worth of over $10,000,000.

Raised in foster homes until her adoption at the age of nine, there was little that made this young girl stand out besides her thick glasses and severe limp. Her elementary school music teachers recalled that she did "okay" in classes, but nothing outstanding. From age 9 to 14 the lower-class working family that adopted her didn't have the money to buy her the violin and music lessons she so desperately desired. Finally, at 14, she began playing the violin. From that moment on she practiced a minimum of two hours a day, and now, at the age of 22, is joyously playing in her city's symphony orchestra and making a comfortable and rewarding living providing violin lessons to children.

• •

At the age of 40, after her third and last child entered elementary school, she decided it was time to work on herself a bit. She had always loved pastries and been interested in baking, but never produced anything more than basic breads, muffins, and pies. In a period of less than eight years she managed to complete an A.A. degree in Culinary Arts, begin her own catering business, specializing in baked goods, win numerous awards for her pastries and cakes, and have her own syndicated column in over 100 newspapers—"The Baking Corner."

A significant helping of motivation can go a long, long way. While it's great to have innate potential and a rich and nurturing environment, most individuals who achieve in this world do so primarily because of their motivation/drive/desire. Their "I will" takes them far further than their IQ.

RECOMMENDATIONS

1. Watch for your children's areas of particular strength (this is also a good idea for areas in need of special attention) and provide them with extra encouragement and stimulation in those areas.

2. In most areas of development one's inheritance allows for a wide range of possible outcomes. Keep an open mind and attitude, maintain optimism, avoid pessimism, and work hard to set up an environment that will help your children grow and learn as much as possible. There's almost certainly more there than you see.

3. The environmental factors critical to your children's development go beyond their physical and academic health and well-being: they also include psychological and social health and well-being. You are a critical ingredient in this. You need to watch yourself and your interactions with your children; being the best you can be will help them to become the best they can be.

4. Many aspects of an individual's potential are more vulnerable to the effects of environment earlier in life. Be cautious about waiting to provide the experiences you think your children will benefit from, such as buying more books, starting gymnastics lessons, providing exposure to a second language, or cutting down on junk food. Consider sooner rather than later, as long as you aren't being too pushy (trying to make them learn things they aren't ready for).

5. Motivation/desire/drive are critical factors in actualizing one's potential. Consider and follow through on strategies to help your children build these very valuable characteristics.

6. Don't just focus on your children's abilities (or disabilities). You may give your all into building their particular area(s) of potential (or disability) and find that despite their potential and the fantastic environment you set up to encourage its development, your goals and theirs weren't met. Children, like adults, usually need to have a balanced life. If too much is devoted to one area at the cost of other areas, specific goals may not be met.

7. Remember that while most of us are dramatically underachieving, compared to who we might be, there never has been and never will be a person who really is an overachiever. Spread the message: MOTIVATION IS GOOD!

SUMMARY

Potential: the ceiling, the limit, the extreme, the very best individuals have in themselves in a given skill, ability, trait or characteristic. While few individuals actually reach this point in any area of their development, many strive for it. Even in the case of "natural genius" (whether it be in an academic pursuit, the arts, or sports), accomplishment and the realization of potential are always accompanied by hard work and usually by excellent instruction and modeling. The unanswerable question is: "What are my children's areas of greatest potential?" Parents often ask themselves, "How far can they go? With time and the right training, what are the limits?" The answer is always the same: "You won't know until you try, and, even then, you may wonder if more might not have been done."

Potential exists in all people, in every area of their existence. Some of the potentially greatest artists of all times never had the opportunity to paint, or play the violin, or learn ballet. Some of the potentially greatest psychotherapists never practiced psychotherapy outside of their own kitchen or with anyone but their own friends and family. The potential was there, waiting and hiding within them, but it never expressed itself fully, and was only shared with a limited audience.

What is the first step in the realization of potential? It's realizing that our children (not to mention ourselves) can be and do a lot more in many areas of life. Parents who are able to focus on this vision are more able to nurture the actualization of that potential in their children. Parents who believe, "Yes, my children are among the worst players on their soccer teams but, with practice, they can be a lot better. Maybe not the best on the team, but absolutely, certainly, undeniably, without any doubt better than they are now." These are the parents who are positioning themselves in the best way to assist their children in the maximization of potential.

The beauty of potential is that every one of us, child and adult, almost certainly could do more and be more with what is already inside of us, with more motivation/drive/desire. So many children just give up: "I can't do computers." "I don't get math." "Nobody likes me." Perceiving themselves at the bottom of the barrel, they determine that is where they are meant to be; that's their destiny. What they are doing is denying their potential, denying that if they decided to make that area more of a priority in their lives, they could be better at it. Once again, maybe not "the best," but certainly better.

CHAPTER 2

ENCOURAGEMENT

INTRODUCTION

Most people use the term *encouragement* to refer to a variety of different approaches, the goal of which is to move children in positive directions, to support or reassure them, and to build their confidence, hope, and internal strength. Encouragement, when used in this way, includes techniques such as positive reinforcement (smiles, praise, rewards), establishing an interesting and motivating environment, making sure that children experience success, providing positive models that they may wish to emulate, allowing for opportunities to use knowledge and skills in real world, useful ways, and a vast array of other strategies.

Throughout this chapter—and the remainder of this book—the word *encouragement* will have this broad, positive meaning.

There is, however, another meaning of the word *encouragement,* a meaning that is related to the more general term just described, but actually just a subset, or small part of it. This more limited type of encouragement, which will be referred to as **en**couragement (with an emphasis on the bold-face **en** to indicate that it is a subset, or part of the more general encouragement) is a technique that attempts to turn the role of reinforcer/supervisor/finder-of-good back on the child. Certainly encouragement and **en**couragement are similar; they both are attempts to help children to achieve more, or feel better about themselves, or in some way become more whole or more accomplished; however, encouragement often does this by setting the adult (or encourager) up as a judge or validator of quality, while **en**couragement requires that children judge themselves.

This chapter will discuss the key ingredients of both encouragement and **en**couragement, as well as their goals:

- to help children feel better about their abilities, efforts, and achievements
- to motivate them to work harder and achieve more
- to enable them to identify and utilize their own strengths

- to assist them in becoming more independent and self-confident
- to teach them to appreciate the process of their efforts as well as the products

---

THE RELEVANCE OF ENCOURAGEMENT IN THE CONTEXT OF THIS BOOK

Being aware that your children have significant potential in a particular area isn't enough. Parents need to have techniques to help bring that potential out—to help actualize it. Parents need to organize environments that keep children actively, productively, creatively, and joyously involved and aware that their efforts have value, and that that value lies both in experiencing the process as well as the product of their efforts.

Encouragement is one of the most powerful tools a parent can use to nurture and bring to life their children's potential.

BASIC ATTITUDES AND TECHNIQUES

Let's start with a list of the basic attitudes and techniques and then go into more detail explaining how you can actually do these things in your everyday life.

Critical *attitudes* to effectively employ encouragement could include the following.

1. Children can often make responsible decisions, and need practice doing so.

2. Children learn more joyously and efficiently when they are learning something that really interests them and with materials that are motivating. (This topic is also discussed in Chapter 5, Emerging Skills.) Parents can try to guide their children and set up environments in which they can learn and grow, but it is the children themselves who must decide what interests and appeals to them and what arouses their passion and desire to learn.

3. A focus on efforts (the process) as well as outcomes (the product) will ultimately yield better products and people who feel more at ease and in tune with themselves and successful at what they do than focusing solely on outcomes.

4. Success, or the feeling of being successful, leads to improved performance and further successes.

Key *techniques* in this social/psychological art form we are calling encouragement are

1. creating an environment with choices, where children can explore and experiment.

2. setting up the environment in such a way that children are challenged, but not frustrated, given the space and opportunity to move to higher levels of understanding and achievement, but not forced to reach predetermined goals.

3. verbally and nonverbally identifying, acknowledging, and helping children to identify and acknowledge (this will later be explained as **en**couragement) their efforts, progress, and the good feelings about themselves that accompany accomplishment.

4. acting as models of those attitudes and behaviors we wish children to develop.

5. providing direct instruction or training when "teachable moments" arise.

Pretty vague so far, isn't it? Don't worry, this section won't end until you know what encouragement and **en**couragement are and have a number of techniques to make them work.

The majority of parents encourage children constantly, and in many ways, such as

■ placing overhead mobiles in babies' cribs. This is encouraging the development of their visual skills and awareness of their environment.

■ taking toddlers to the park. This is encouraging them to enjoy and appreciate the outdoors (assuming that it's a pleasant experience and you model enjoyment and appreciation!) and develops their coordination.

- reading an interesting and engaging story or book to children who want to be read to. This is encouraging their language development and desire to read.
- expressing your enjoyment and excitement in the pursuit of hobbies and areas of interest is encouraging them to develop hobbies and interests.
- providing children with environments and activities that are interesting, motivating, and challenging. This encourages them to become involved, to experience, and to experiment.
- listening to them as they share their attitudes and beliefs, making an honest effort to understand them, and accepting what they believe and say. This encourages them to investigate and learn more about themselves.

As can be seen from the above examples, encouragement is a broad topic with many subtle nuances. For those of you who have been raised in encouraging environments, many aspects of encouraging children seem to come as easily and naturally as breathing or walking, but for those who themselves have received less of this type of attention, the skills are a bit more difficult to build, yet still well worth the effort.

Keep in mind when considering the use of encouragement that one of its primary goals is to place more responsibility for decision making and progress on your children, rather than on yourself. This is particularly true of **en**couragement, which hasn't been explained well yet, but believe me, it's coming. Encouragement is not bribing, threatening, coercing, pushing, or pulling children so they'll accomplish a certain goal or reach a certain level of achievement. It's not that directive or specific goal-oriented. It's not the old behavior modification system of rewards and punishments, designed to make children change behaviors or develop specific skills, although rewards can at times be regarded as encouraging in some ways. Encouragement is far more subtle than all that. What it does is set up an environment where children's abilities and special areas of interest will be acknowledged, ever so gently nourished, and given an excellent opportunity to emerge and blossom.

Buying into this system may require you to change one or more of your basic paradigms, or mind-sets, on child rearing. To utilize this system you may need to back off a bit from what and who you want your children to be, and open up a bit more to allowing them to be or become, to express and actualize, what is within them. The more you use the encouragement system the more your children's energy and desires will be open to their own self-expression, rather than their being dominated by serving others and the goals that have been set *for them.* If your children do not become involved in an activity or interest that you'd like them involved in, if they don't show an interest, don't push, or bribe, or threaten. (Well, you can still do these things, but then you've moved to other techniques that are not part of encouragement.) By encouraging, you merely set things up, or create an atmosphere or environment. For example:

You may force your children to sit and practice the piano, but if they don't like the piano or don't want to learn the lessons and don't want to practice, the experience will more likely lead to a negative attitude and resentment than to beautiful music and enjoyment of the art. On the other hand, encouraging your children to study piano by buying one, playing it yourself, paying attention when they attempt to play, going to piano concerts, or discussing the melodies or sounds your children enjoy, greatly increases the chances that your children will decide to study the piano. Even if they decide not to study the piano, at the very least these encouraging experiences will have provided them with some excellent enrichment and no harm has been done.

• •

You may try to teach young children to throw and catch, and, despite their lack of interest, make them work with you on those skills for extended periods of time. This may, if you're lucky, help them learn to throw and catch better. These same goals, however, would very probably be easier to accomplish, and surpass, with other approaches. More encouraging, and probably successful approaches would be starting a game of catch with two or three children at once (add a social element), perhaps with a noncompetitive game format (more motivation) for short periods of time (less taxing and demanding), possibly with a goal or outcome in mind: "After we do ten throws and catches in a row, let's jump up in the air together and scream, okay?" Use frequent fun rewards and breaks.

You may, if you wish, establish 30-minute tutoring sessions with your five-year-olds, focusing on the recognition of ABCs, beginning sounds, and reading simple words. For some young children this may be fun and motivating, and may teach them the basics of reading, but it is also possible that children may learn to hate reading if it is introduced in this way, and clashes may develop. The same 30 minutes spent with less goal direction but still involved with letters and words and sounds— encouraging, rather than pushing—may not teach as many specific skills, but may well entice them more into the world of reading. By encouraging them to delve deeper, they will eventually be led to higher levels of proficiency.

Encouragement is a technique that can be used occasionally in unison with other techniques, or a philosophy that can serve as the primary tool to lead children into deep and rewarding investigations and new learning, and help them develop a multitude of skills and abilities.

One goal of this book is to provide parents with many techniques to encourage. It is up to you whether these techniques and the philosophy that underlies them will become the mainstay of your interactions with your children, or whether additional techniques, used occasionally, can enhance your relationship and their learning.

Now, let's look more closely at the specific attitudes and techniques involved in encouragement.

SPECIFIC ATTITUDES

1. Children can often make responsible decisions, and need practice doing so.

A fairly common view is that it takes many years for children to become responsible decision makers. People who believe this would probably say that during the first few years of children's lives (some regard this period as lasting until "children" turn 18 or 21 years old. I think my parents perceived me as a child until I myself became a parent, at the age of 39!), parents need to make many or most important decisions for their children. This theory holds that as children grow older they can begin to take more charge of their own lives, and play a greater role in determining their destinies. By the age of 18 or 21 these children will have had thousands of decisions made for them and will therefore have learned how to make their own decisions.

Now, I'll agree that there are many decisions adults should probably *not* put in the hands of children, such as the following examples.

Parent to six-month-old: "Give Mommy the rock, Honey. We don't eat rocks. Here, would you like to chew on this teether instead?"

Parent to two-year-old: "Yes, throwing all the pillows into the fire would make it bigger, but we don't want to burn up the pillows. Here's a piece of wood. Would you like to throw it into the fire?"

Parent to four-year-old: "I know you want to have a milk shake and chocolate cake for dinner, but let's save our dessert for the end of the meal and start with some protein and vegetables. Would you prefer chicken or fish? A salad or soup?" (I am aware that some very prominent parenting and nutrition experts warn about using desserts as rewards, but I have been unable to rid myself of this old habit. Some of these same parenting and nutrition experts are also convinced that, if allowed to eat as they liked, children would naturally balance their own diets. Once again, I am stuck in tradition and personally find this very hard to believe.)

Parent to six-year-old: "You're right, the baby probably would make a great big splash if we threw her into the swimming pool, but she might also drown. Now, bring the baby off the diving board very slowly. No, no, no, carry her, don't drag her! Good job. How about if you and I jump up and down in the water and make big splashes?"

Parent to seven-year-old: "Yes, I know you want to drive the car. How about helping me with the shifting? Here, put your hand on the gear shifter and when I put the clutch in we'll move it together."

Parent to eight-year-old: "I know you want to fight with Charlie, but we don't do that when we have friends over for the day. We've got to talk about what's going on with you guys. Do you want to discuss it here in the yard, or would you rather go inside and talk about it over a lemonade?"

Parents can and should tell their children "No" at times—quickly and decisively state that a particular behavior or idea is unacceptable; however, parents should consider, whenever possible, engaging in a bit more open and elaborative dialogue with their children. Rather than merely saying, "No," which can be quite discouraging, look at the needs children are expressing and try to meet those needs in positive (encouraging) ways that help teach and model acceptable behavior.

Related to this, we the parents should not give children choices when they really don't have a choice. In other words, don't ask questions like these when you really mean to state a demand.

Would you like to hit Daddy a few more times?

Do you think you'll be going to bed tonight?

Do you think you want to clean up that milk you just spilled on the floor?

We need to leave for school right now or we're going to be late. Do you want to get in the car?

Are you going to brush your teeth or am I going to stand here all night waiting for you? (Just the thought of this question leads my sick little brain in a thousand creative, sarcastic directions.)

These questions sound silly, don't they? Silly, yes, but all too often I hear parents asking questions like these. (I like to limit myself to 10 to 20 dumb questions a day!)

Therefore, don't ask a question when your real message is an order or demand!

We should not give children choices when they really don't have a choice, but, we should and must give them as many opportunities as possible to make decisions, to use their own judgment, to weigh facts and feelings and preferences, and to enjoy or suffer the consequences (see a further discussion of consequences in Chapter 3) of their decisions. Not all the time—not in situations where they really aren't going to be allowed to decide, but as often as seems reasonable, and regarding both little, less important decisions, as well as larger, more long-term and significant life-planning alternatives.

"Examples, give me examples," you say. Okay. But, remember, if you aren't accustomed to allowing children to make many decisions for themselves, you'll want to start slowly. Experiment and practice with this technique and see how it suits you. If you like it, if it feels right, keep doing it and observe how it works and the benefits it provides. If it doesn't work for you right away, don't give up. Change is rarely easy. Give yourself time—years in fact—to work on this skill. I've been practicing this technique for decades and still have lots of room for growth. Now here are some examples of what you *should* do.

Mother to three-day-old daughter: "Well, Sweetie, want some of Mommy's milk?" Baby makes a sound. Mommy says, "Sounds like a Yes to me. Here you go."

Father to an energetic, physical, "I feel like breaking something" two-year-old: "So Mister, would you rather play wrestle or play kick the ball?"

Parent and five-year-old at county fair: "Let's see, you brought $5 of your own money and here's $5 more I want you to have fun with. You can pick the rides you want to go on and the games you want to play, but remember, when you run out of money, you're done."

Parents to a seven- and an eight-year-old: "Let's each write down the names of three restaurants we'd like to go to for dinner and we'll see what we come up with."

> *Mother to a dawdling eight-year-old:* "You're going to be in bed with the lights out in 10 minutes. You choose if you want to spend that 10 minutes looking at your toothbrush and avoiding brushing or lying with Mommy in bed while she tells you a story."

There are a number of ways to provide children with the opportunity to make a decision.

1. Deciding between two or perhaps three choices that are supplied to them: milk or juice?

2. Having them list or think of their possible choices and then select: "What do you think you want to write your story about? Which topic do you want to start on?"

3. Asking an all-in-one question, where they consider their choices and make a decision without assistance. "You're going to Amanda's party Saturday. We need to buy her a present. I'm willing to spend up to $12, but you need to tell me what you want to bring her."

Our goal is to help children learn to make responsible decisions with as little help as possible. If they are doing this already, great! Give them many opportunities to practice and succeed. If they are having difficulty, we need to structure situations, as in #1 and #2 above, where they can feel successful and competent.

2. Children learn more joyously and efficiently when they are learning something that really interests them and with materials that are motivating.

(This topic is also discussed in Chapter 5, Emerging Skills.) It's much easier to get children involved in activities that interest them, rather than activities that interest only us or that we want to force them to be interested in.

■ To encourage children to become more involved in music, let them select the instrument they want to play (including their own voice), and the type of music they wish to learn.

- To encourage children to read more, assist them in selecting books that interest them, at difficulty levels they can handle. For books they read to themselves, they should be able to read 85 to 90+ percent of the words fairly smoothly and fluently.

- To encourage children to learn a new sport, watch for their interests and ask them what sports they'd like to learn. Then respect their choices and provide them with opportunities.

- To encourage children to help with chores around the house, make a list of all the jobs that need to be done and give them some say in determining which jobs will be their responsibility.

- To encourage children to practice their math facts, have them think of games that could be used as mediums for practice, or materials (like jelly beans or real money) that might be used as tangible, physical aids.

There are many different ways in which children can gain mastery of different skills, and many different materials that can be utilized in the process. By allowing your children a voice in the determination of personal learning goals and objectives, as well as the ways they'll get there and the materials that will assist them, you can encourage them to become more involved, and motivate them toward success.

3. Focus on efforts (the process), as well as outcomes (the product).

Focusing on efforts and outcomes will ultimately yield better products and will result in children who feel more at ease and in tune with themselves and successful at what they do, than focusing solely on outcomes.

When involved in projects or various endeavors we—children and adults—all too often lose sight of the joy, peace, and fulfillment our efforts bring us, while focusing too much on the products or outcomes. In an effort to finish or complete something, we sometimes don't pay enough attention to, or appreciate, the ingredients we put in. For example:

After playing a fantastic game, and scoring three goals, a six-year-old runs off the field crying because the match has been lost.

A five-year-old has spent ten minutes joyously coloring a picture and then gets upset after making one stray mark on the paper. Rather than look at the good parts of the picture and the joy experienced while coloring it, the child can only focus on the stray mark and the flawed product.

A four-year-old is so concerned about having someone watch her attempt a cartwheel, and praise her for it, that she rushes through the movements and completes a less-than-best performance, just to hear the compliments.

An eight-year-old much too quickly reads the directions for building a model airplane because he's anxious to see what the model will look like when completed, and ends up missing some critical directions and having a product that doesn't look very good.

While there's nothing wrong with wanting to win or to create something beautiful, or to be watched, or to finish something, there is a problem when we lose sight of the attention to detail, efforts, and enjoyment of the processes that are required to produce our best results.

As parents, we need to acknowledge our children's efforts, not just the results of those efforts. We need to reflect to them our awareness that they are trying hard, and assist them in building self-observation and reflection skills that they can utilize to monitor their own progress and growth.

We want our children to grow into adults who will feel good about their tennis game, whether they win or lose, who will enjoy reading, whether or not they remember every little detail they've read, who will feel good about their singing or playing an instrument, regardless of how others respond to them, or whether or not they make money from it, and who will look in the mirror and like how they look, rather than be overly concerned about how others will see or perceive them.

4. Success, or the feeling of being successful, leads to improved performance and further successes.

For most people, failure is discouraging and success is encouraging. Some individuals can handle repeated failures and still maintain a positive "I can do" attitude, while others give up at the first feelings of failure. As parents, two of our more important jobs are (1) setting up environments where our children can experience the feeling of success, and (2) teaching them that we don't always succeed on our first try, and just because our goals have not yet been achieved, that doesn't mean that they never will be reached.

The sink-or-swim/don't-make-it-too-easy-for-them attitude that some parents may have regarding building skills and self-confidence in their children may work for some, but is not a good general rule or principle to follow. A much more reliable and productive attitude is success leads to more success/set your children up for success.

- A young child should learn to count to 20 before learning to count by twos.
- Most four- and five-year-olds need to practice riding bicycles with the training wheels on before taking the wheels off.
- A child who has difficulty remembering to follow two directions (such as, "Go and brush your teeth and then put on your pajamas") should more often be given single directions and learn from the experience of repeated successes, rather than be pushed to follow three or four directions at a time.
- A seven-year-old needs to learn to ice-skate before joining a competitive ice hockey team.
- A third grader who struggles reading second grade level books should be provided with slightly easier books, perhaps at the first grade level, rather than be pushed to read the third grade-level books that some of the other children in the class are reading.

The attitude of one-step-at-a-time, move-from-easier-to-harder, build-on-successes, make-sure-they-can-do-the-basics before-introducing-harder-more-complex tasks, when necessary, drop-back-and-reteach/relearn-unmastered-steps-before-going-on attitude will encourage your children to continue trying and learning. Be patient—it's better to move ahead a bit more slowly than to move too quickly and eventually give up because of failure and frustration.

SPECIFIC TECHNIQUES

1. Create an environment with choices, where children can explore and experiment.

- If your six-year-olds demonstrate an interest or potential in studying and learning about insects and animals, take them to science fairs, exhibits, and zoos; provide them with books, games, computer programs, and videos; enroll them in extracurricular classes and activities.
- If your eight-year-olds seem to have an interest or potential in understanding their feelings and emotions or the feelings and emotions of others, read and discuss books that deal with emotions and relationships; encourage them to join different types of social groups; assist them in learning how to keep a journal.
- If your three-year-olds enjoy numbers, counting, and working with blocks and geometric shapes, or seem to have potential in that area, buy or collect different types of blocks, tangrams, and objects of different sizes and shapes for them to play with; involve them in counting, classifying, and sorting games; try to use logical/mathematical-type reasoning when explaining things to them.
- If your four-year-olds love painting, drawing, and playing with Play-Doh and clay, set up an art table in the basement, garage, or back room and have lots of art materials they can explore and create with.

Your home is the first and most important learning environment your children will ever experience. The richer and

more varied that environment is, the greater the chances that
your children will realize their potential. You don't need to be
wealthy to accomplish this.

● ●

Rocks, twigs, and leaves from outside are every bit as
good as, if not better than, purchased games and activities
that are designed to teach sorting and classifying skills.

Library books work just as well as books purchased at a
store.

Free-of-charge, community enrichment programs can
often stimulate learning in a new field as much as expen-
sive tutors or privately run programs.

A $50 garage sale saxophone and a $1 used instruction
book will take a motivated young musician much further
than a $2,000, top-of-the-line, silver saxophone and $30
an hour lessons will take a child who isn't interested in
music or doesn't have much potential.

● ●

2. Set up an environment in which children are challenged but not frustrated, given the space and opportunity to move to higher levels of understanding and achievement but not forced to reach predetermined goals.

This topic is also discussed in Chapter 5, Emerging Skills.
When educators and psychologists consider what materials or
assignments are appropriate for young learners, they usually
conceptualize three different categories or levels of difficulty:

■ Independent level. A child is able to perform successfully at approximately the 85 to 90+ percent level—
very few errors and little stumbling over not quite mastered skills—with no assistance.

■ Instructional level. A child is able to perform successfully at approximately the 75 to 85 percent level—
some errors and stumbling over not quite mastered
skills—but, assistance to correct errors and provide
instruction is readily available.

■ Frustration level. A child is able to perform successfully below the 70 to 75 percent level—this is regarded as too difficult, too frustrating for most children, even if assistance is readily available.

These levels apply most importantly to involvement in learning tasks that have right and wrong answers, such as fitting game or puzzle pieces together, matching games and activities (r goes with R, b goes with B, 4 goes with IV), reading, spelling, math computations, and answering questions orally and in writing. The reasoning behind these percentages is that if the tasks are too hard the young learners will either become overly frustrated or make so many errors that they will become even more uncertain and confused.

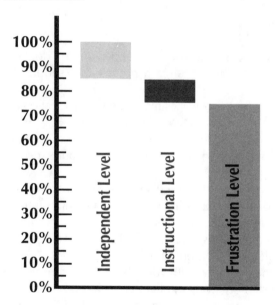

For students with special learning needs (learning disabilities, emotional or behavioral difficulties, developmental disabilities/mental retardation, histories of failure) we usually raise the percentages a bit; they need to experience more success. For students who are gifted or very motivated, we sometimes consider lowering these percentages; they can often deal with and sometimes thrive from more challenge.

The key points here are that some materials and tasks are appropriate for children to become engaged in without assistance (children are at the 85 to 90+ percent mastery level). Others are appropriate but only when assistance is readily available (75 to 85 percent mastery). Still others are too difficult, even when assistance is readily available (below 70 to 75 percent mastery).

"Of course, obviously!" you say. However, how obvious is this to parents who sit down to help their seven-year-olds read books in which 50 percent of the words require parental help? Or to parents who give their four-year-olds small pads of paper and handfuls of marking pens and then become upset at them for marking up the kitchen table? Or to parents of eight-year-olds, who are having difficulty multiplying single-digit numbers, yet attempt to teach their children how to multiply two digits times two digits?! You can't "put the cart before the horse."

The "Shoulds"

Enough of what you can't and shouldn't do. Let's look at what you probably are already doing—the "shoulds."

- Keep the percentages mentioned in this section (85 to 90+ percent = independent level; 75 to 85 percent = instructional level; <70 or 75 percent = frustration level) in mind, and make an effort to keep your expectations reasonable.
- Be aware of those skills your children are in the process of mastering (85 to 90+ percent on their own) and try to surround them with experiences and materials that are right at that level and, when help is available, slightly more difficult.
- When working with your children, be sensitive to their frustration level, and lighten or ease up when their frustration mounts. Make the tasks more difficult (in small increments) if they seem to be too easy or they're becoming boring.

Following are some examples of how to put these ideas into practice and how to be flexible or adapt once you realize that you've erred.

If you're working on flash cards with your children, and they miss two or three in a row, make an effort to "stack the deck" to ensure that they then get a number of easy questions; build their confidence back up.

If your children need and want new bikes, get them the right size so they can control them better and be more successful at riding, thus lowering the chances of an accident, rather than getting them a larger size because it will last longer.

If your children really want to read a book to you and it turns out that they can only read about 50 to 75 percent of the words on their own, don't correct them if they misread a word yet are able to maintain the integrity or meaning of the sentence.

If your young children are interested in science and want microscopes, start with ones made for young children with knobs that are easy to grasp, manipulate, and focus, rather than more complicated microscopes that they will have difficulty operating.

If your four-year-olds are able to catch and throw a 10-inch ball with relative ease (85+ percent), then buy an 8-inch ball (a bit more difficult) and play with that. If their proficiency drops down too much (below 70 to 75 percent) and they seem to become frustrated or become less interested, then go back to the 10-inch ball, or use the 8-inch ball, but get closer together—make it easier! Remember, all the percentages mentioned in this section are averages and may need to be adjusted for your children.

Think back to the story of the tortoise and the hare. The fast-moving hare "burned out," and some say never even finished the race, while the tortoise moved at her own speed, kept up a slow but steady pace, and surpassed the goals anyone might have set for her!

3. Verbally and nonverbally identify and acknowledge their efforts, progress, and the good thoughts and feelings that accompany accomplishment.

Many parents and professionals regard this technique as a key variable in the art of encouragement. I think you'll be able to handle the confusion here—the same word meaning two different things. Remember, if the word **en**couragement begins with **en**, it means the specific technique being described in this section; if encouragement does not start with a bold en, then it means all the different things we do to motivate children and keep them involved and learning, including the specific technique of **en**couragement.

Praise Versus **En**couragement

The best place to begin the explanation of this technique is through a comparison and contrast with a word you are already familiar with—praise. Praise is a verbal form of positive reinforcement and one of many ways in which we encourage children; praisers in some way compliment or point out something they like, something they think is positive and worthwhile.

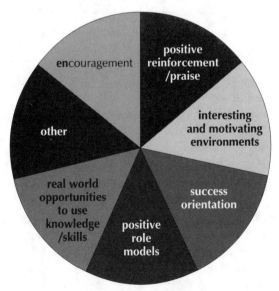

Encouragement

Encouragement is similar to praise, but with a difference.

> Praise *usually comes* after *the act or project is complet-ed and is used more to positively reinforce or encourage the end result.*
>
> **En**couragement *comes* throughout *one's involve-ment in an act or project and is meant to encourage the end result, but, more important, to encourage the* process *involved regardless of the end result.*

The praiser is the judge, while the **en**courager sets children up as their own judges.

> Praise *is best when it is specific, when the children being praised are told exactly what they did well.*
>
> **En**couragement *is best when it is more subtle or vague and children are made to evaluate themselves.*

Personally speaking, I've been aware of these differences for more than 20 years and have been making a concerted effort to praise less and **en**courage more (but I believe in using loads of both). Those of you who decide to experiment with this approach/technique must be patient with yourselves. If you, as I, have been raised with more praise than **en**couragement, it will require constant attention and effort to move your behavior to this new way, a way many hope and believe will lead children to more self-awareness and independence, higher levels of achievement, and a strong sense of responsibility.

Before giving examples of **en**couraging statements and actions, let me say that the key to whether or not your statement or action is **en**couragement, rather than praise, is in how it is perceived by children. If your statement or action motivates chil-dren to look within themselves—to self-evaluate, judge their own effort and work, and want to continue and improve to please and improve themselves—then you actually did **en**courage. If howev-er, what you say or do leaves children thinking, "Mom likes it;

therefore it's good" or, "I pleased Dad; therefore I did well," then despite your intent to **en**courage, you somehow missed. Don't feel bad though, because you may not have **en**couraged, but you did praise, which is a technique you'll almost certainly want to continue to use. It's like shooting a basketball—you can't look at the shooter's form or follow-through and tell if it's a successful shot; you can't necessarily listen to the words or watch the actions of the **en**courager to know if they **en**couraged. You have to wait and see whether or not the ball goes in the basket; you have to see how the children being **en**couraged perceive your words or actions—if the result is that they evaluate and approve of themselves then you were successful.

Here are some examples:

A ten-month-old is trying to take a step, and keeps falling down and trying again.

Praise: "Fantastic, you're going to be walking and running all over soon," or "Great job, Honey, your balance is getting so good," or "Mommy is so proud of you."

Encouragement: "Well young man, your smile tells me you're pretty proud of yourself" or "Oh my, look at that determination in your face; you're just going to keep on trying, aren't you?!" or "Come to Mommy" (and Mom places her hands close enough that he can walk to her, but far enough away so as to challenge his sense of balance)—and then smile when he walks to you.

A four-year-old runs up to Mom and says, "Look at my picture."

Praise: "Beautiful job, Honey," or "I love it," or "You're a great artist."

Encouragement: "What do you like about it?," or "You sure worked hard on this, didn't you?!," or "Oh my..." (and then silence—waiting for the child to add her thoughts or feelings).

A seven-year-old is sitting at the computer playing an addition and subtraction game.

Praise: "What a smart little girl you are," or "You're doing a great job, Sweetie," or "Daddy's little computer whiz."

Encouragement: "You really seem to be having fun," or "What are your favorite parts of this program?," or just

> *watch and be silent and wait for the child to talk (your just being there, and watching her may be encouraging).*
>
> •
>
> *An eight-year-old is reading aloud a very difficult book about the creation of the universe. She is trying hard, but having some difficulty.*
>
> *Praise:* "Great reading," or "Nice job," or "You must be the best reader in your class."
>
> *Encouragement:* "You like to pick hard books that really push you to your max," or "If you can read this book you can read anything—this has a lot of big words," or "You usually pick science books to read to me. What is it you like so much about science?"

There's nothing wrong with praise, when used prudently. It usually helps motivate children and often makes them feel better about themselves and their accomplishments. By the way, don't forget that the best praise is specific; it tells children exactly what it is they have done well/what you like.

General Praise Versus Specific Praise

In my mind general praise is okay; specific praise is better. (Actually, when teaching certain skills, specific praise is a very

PRAISE	
SPECIFIC	**GENERAL**
I love the way you drew it with such lively, bright colors.	Nice job.
Great follow-through on your throw. I like the way you pulled your back leg around.	Good throw.
You put such emotion and excitement in your voice. It makes the story really come alive.	Excellent reading.

useful and wonderful tool, telling kids exactly what they are doing correctly!) But **en**couragement is best. I believe that each has its place in child rearing and should be used freely and guiltlessly. If our real goal is to raise children who strive to do their best, rather than merely meet the standards set for them, **en**couragement is usually a more effective and appropriate tool than praise. If we want to focus more on teaching our children to evaluate and appreciate their own efforts, rather than be dependent on the evaluations of others and only feel successful when they win or are recognized for their achievements, then we need to practice this subtle and powerful technique called **en**couragement.

4. Act as models of those attitudes and behaviors you wish children to develop.

This will be a short section because the topic is covered in much more depth in Chapter 6, Modeling. However, it also fits under the topic of encouragement (we're back to the general, all inclusive encouragement, again).

While you don't have to be or do something yourself for your children to learn to be or do it, it often helps. When children see a parent exemplifying a trait or skill that they themselves have thought of developing, they not only are provided with a model, but also are encouraged because (1) many children wish to be like their parents, and (2) you probably can do it much better than they can, at least while they're still young— enjoy this while you can!—and they can see what their own practice and perseverance may lead to.

When your children see you grabbing every free minute to dive into a novel or magazine or journal or newspaper, they tend to respect reading more and want to read. When you exercise regularly and exemplify a love of movement, staying in shape, and pushing your body to peak performance, they tend to want to do the same, and think that that's what a body is for. When they observe you being a kind and loving person, helping friends and being involved in your community, they naturally assume that's what a person does, and are encouraged to be more caring, sensitive, and involved. While this tendency to model on parents is not a hard-and-fast rule, it's something we need to be aware of and a phenomenon that can help remind us to be the best we, their parents, can be!

5. Provide direct instruction or training when "teachable moments" arise.

Once again, this topic will be covered in Chapter 9, Tutoring Techniques, but it also fits in well under encouragement, so a few words need to be said about it right here and now. Another way of encouraging our children is by being effective guides or helpers in their learning. If we're sensitive about when and how to help them, keeping the focus on them as the ones who are responsible for their own learning, they will be encouraged to continue putting out the effort that is required to get the most they can from their potential.

Some useful techniques include

- helping children to identify and correct their own errors.
- providing them with activities and learning challenges at which they can succeed, but that are not too easy.
- using as many settings and opportunities as possible to reinforce learning (such as in the car, during bath time, while cooking supper, or on walks).
- assisting them to identify and appreciate their own growth and new learning.

These techniques and more will be discussed in Chapter 9, and all, when used appropriately, can reinforce your children's progress toward maximizing their potential.

RECOMMENDATIONS

1. Continue praising your children, but also experiment with the technique of **en**couragement. This is a skill that needs to be practiced and evaluated in order to do it well.

2. Make an effort to get your children to evaluate their own performance, to be their own supporters and critics.

3. Provide your children with as many opportunities as possible, starting from birth, to make decisions and evaluate the decisions they have made.

4. Remember to pay attention to the process, not just the result of your children's efforts. Help them learn to appreciate the process, not just the result or outcome.

5. Remember that most children need to succeed at the 85 to 90+ percent level at least when working independently, that below 70 or 75 percent success, even with a teacher or tutor right by their side, most children experience a feeling of failure, and that the ideal level where instruction (with a knowledgeable helper present) should occur is between these two levels.

6. Follow your children's interests, and use those interests to incorporate new learning in their lives.

7. As your children's most significant role models, be what you hope your children will someday be.

8. Set your children up for success; success leads to more success; failure leads to failure.

SUMMARY

F or the potential our children possess to be realized we must
make every effort to encourage them in every way possible.
Some individuals are magically able to accomplish incredible things despite their environments; however, without the
guidance of caring and competent mentors (which can be us,
the parents), most individuals fall far short of what might have
been their "best." To help our children reach and use more of
what they have inside them, we need to assist them in learning
who and what they are, and what they like and are good at
(**en**couragement is one of our strongest allies here). We need to
set up environments that challenge them, lead them to experience success, acknowledge their efforts, and teach them to
acknowledge themselves. We need to provide them with models
of excellence and visions of what their efforts might someday
achieve and who they may become.

CHAPTER 3

CONSEQUENCES
VERSUS
PUNISHMENT

INTRODUCTION

Consequences and punishment are both responses to undesired actions or misbehavior. The purpose or use of both is to diminish the frequency or intensity (in other words, to *stop!*) those actions or that misbehavior. The primary difference between the two is that consequences are related in some way to the action or misbehavior, while punishments usually are not. (Keep in mind throughout this section that many people use the two terms interchangeably; however, for the purposes of this chapter and book, they are very different!) The primary goal of this section is to encourage parental use of consequences in dealing with undesired actions and misbehavior and to discourage the use of punishment.

THE RELEVANCE OF CONSEQUENCES VERSUS PUNISHMENT IN THE CONTEXT OF THIS BOOK

Consequences, as opposed to punishment, teach children to look within themselves, rather than to others, when considering their actions and the effects those actions may have. Consequences are also far better teachers of responsibility than are punishments. In order for parents to do the most they can at the job of encouraging potential in their children, they must help them, in every way possible, to learn to look within themselves and be responsible for their decisions, actions, and the results of what they do.

Unlike rewards, praise, and encouragement, the primary goal of which is to increase the frequency or likelihood of a desirable behavior, the primary goal of consequences and punishment is to stop or decrease the frequency or likelihood of an undesirable behavior. Before moving into the subject of consequences versus punishment, you should be informed that neither work nearly as well, or as consistently, as rewards, praise, and encouragement. Put another way, it's usually easier to get someone to continue doing something or do it more often (through rewards, praise, and encouragement) than it is to stop them from doing something or make them do it less often (through consequences and punishment). Now, back to punishment and consequences.

■ What is punishment and what's wrong with it?
■ What are consequences and what's right about them?
■ How do consequences help encourage potential in children?

Read on for the exciting answers to these important questions and learn how to develop a powerful technique (consequences) that will lessen negative and hurtful feelings between you and your children and lead them to a deeper understanding of their place in society and the family and a more responsible and cooperative life.

WHAT IS PUNISHMENT AND WHAT'S WRONG WITH IT?

L et's begin with *punishment.* Most of us have experienced it and we know that it can work very quickly to discourage undesired behaviors, that is, if we think the "punisher" will find out! We also know that it can lead to hurt feelings, anger, damaged relationships, and feelings and thoughts that life isn't fair or just or friendly. First, some examples:

One-year-olds spill milk; you yell or get angry.

Three-year-olds say, "I hate you!"; you slap them on the bottom. (I personally never have and never will slap my daughter on the bottom or on any part of her body; I don't believe in it, but I know some parents believe in this form of punishment.)

Four-year-olds break dishes; you send them to their rooms.

Five-year-olds hit another child; they don't get to go to the movies on Saturday.

Seven-year-olds go wild in their bedroom and leave a mess; they get no dessert after dinner.

When children do or say something you don't like, you proceed to "teach them a lesson" by creating an unrelated (punishments may sometimes be related to the misbehavior they are meant to discourage, but are often or usually not) negative experience for them to go through. Your children are supposed to learn to not do or say what they did or said, and the fear of the punishment is supposed to be what stops them. The good news is that punishment often works and is the quickest way to temporarily stop an undesired behavior. Out of fear that a punishment will be inflicted upon them, many, or perhaps most, children will avoid doing or saying certain things *when authority figures are near.* (It's something like us grownups not speeding in our cars when we think there might be an officer of the law around!) The bad news?

1. Punishment is based on fear—do we really want to raise children to be afraid of us? If your answer to this question is "Yes, I want my children to fear me," then be warned that discipline through fear may sometimes seem to work, with younger children, but almost always becomes less effective as children get older. It tends to create a distance or an invisible wall between parents and children. Arbitrary punishments—and punishments very often do seem arbitrary to children, as if they are based on parental whim—can damage both the children's self concepts and also relationships

with their parents. In addition to these problems, as children become older, as they grow into adolescence, the "fear me" technique often leads to defiance, resentment, and, in general, breaks down into a chaotic series of power struggles and bickering—it doesn't work!

2. Punishments work much better when the punisher observes the misdeed and acts quickly and decisively. The longer you wait before punishing, the less meaning and effect the punishment has. Do we really want to watch every move our children make, and constantly pounce on them when they misbehave? (If your answer to this question is "Yes," it is highly recommended that you get a life!)

3. Punishments often need to intensify (louder screaming, harder spankings, longer groundings, for example) in order to remain effective. How far will you go to stop behavior you don't approve of? How loud will you yell? How hard will you spank? How long will you put them under restriction, or in time-out, or keep them grounded? (I'm sadly reminded of a mother who once told me that she had just grounded her 12-year-old daughter for an entire year. I asked why and she said, "Well, at first we tried just a few minutes, and that didn't work. Then we tried an hour, and that didn't work. We then started grounding her for days, and then weeks, and then months. As soon as the groundings were finished she'd go right back and do the same old things she was grounded for. This time she'll see that we really mean business!" What do you think? Is this mom onto a hot idea? A usable technique? I think not! My advice would be to consider another approach.)

4. Punishment does little to create internal responsibility and maturity. Children are less likely to develop strong internal monitoring systems (see Chapter 7, Responsibility) to help them determine appropriate versus inappropriate behavior and right versus wrong when raised in a system based on punishment. Do we want children to merely behave, or to also develop an internal sense of right and wrong, of appropriate and inappropriate behavior?

So, what are you to do if you can't punish your children for breaking something, or making a mess, or coming home late, or bad language? How can you do your job of helping to socialize them? How can you teach them what's acceptable and unacceptable in our society? The answer is *consequences*.

WHAT ARE CONSEQUENCES AND WHAT'S RIGHT ABOUT THEM?

Similar in some ways to punishment, but fundamentally very different, consequences are one of your strongest allies in the struggle against chaos and barbarism. What are consequences? Well, they are like punishment in that after your children misbehave, or perhaps have a careless accident, something undesirable happens, something that will decrease the likelihood of their doing or saying that same thing again. However, consequences are different in that they must be related to the misdeed, and, ideally, your children will understand the relationship between what they did and the consequence that followed. Let's look at some examples of consequences. Please keep in mind that most misbehavior has a multitude of possible consequences that a parent might utilize—you are limited only by your own creativity.

Eighteen-month-olds spill milk from their cups. What's the consequence? Let's think. Perhaps they won't get tippy cups next time, but bottles instead. Perhaps they won't get any more milk with their lunch. Perhaps they'll now have to drink water instead, and they don't like water. There are many possible consequences for just about any situation. For now, let's make the consequence cleaning up their own mess, or at least making an effort to. True, with their assistance the mess might become even bigger. It may spread from the table to the floors to the walls to their clothes to the cat and dog, but don't think about that—focus on what's being learned here. "What's being learned?" you ask. Your children are beginning to learn about rational, logical, real-world cause-and-effect relationships ("Make a mess → Clean it up"). They are forming responsibility, self-sufficiency, and independence. They may also be driving you crazy, but at least they are learning to clean up after themselves.

Three-year-olds say "I hate you!" What's the consequence? Let's think. Perhaps you'll send them to their room ("If you can't treat people nicely, then you can't be with people!"). Or perhaps a consequence might be, "Well then, I don't want to fold the laundry with someone who hates me. I take back the offer of letting you help!" Or perhaps a look of disapproval, a scowl, a face that says, "When someone is mean to me, I don't respond by being sweet and nice." Again, there are many possible consequences for just about any situation. For now, let's make the consequence removing yourself from the immediate situation and discussing the episode with them at a later time. The children will see that when they act in certain ways, people may not want to be around them. They also are provided with the opportunity to discuss the matter but only after they have calmed down and are ready to treat you with the respect you deserve.

• •

Eight-year-olds carelessly break a nice dish, while showing off a trick. What's the consequence? Let's think. Perhaps it's decided that the broken dish was their dish, and until further notice they'll have to eat off paper plates or maybe use the "baby plates" they feel they have grown out of. Or perhaps a consequence might be that they glue the plate back together and it will be their dinner plate for a time. There are usually many possible consequences to consider. For this situation let's select the consequence that they clean up the mess and, with money from their piggy bank, go to the store with you and buy a replacement dish. The lesson: "If we take chances in life, we need to be prepared to pay for the results."

• •

Seven-year-olds go wild in their bedroom and leave a mess. I know, you know, there are lots of possible consequences to invent here, so, let's cut to the chase and say that those toys and clothing items left scattered about are removed from the room and placed in temporary storage for a number of days, during which time the children do not have access to them. The message: "Abuse it and lose it," "Take care of it or it's taken away."

Of course, the preceding consequences are only examples. In most situations there are dozens, perhaps hundreds, of possible consequences for every misbehavior. I enjoy asking children their ideas for consequences. Here are the key ingredients.

- ■ The consequence must be related to the misbehavior in a way that children can understand.
- ■ Children should feel that through the consequence they have "made things right," that they have helped correct the situation.
- ■ The consequence will assist your children in developing their own sense of right and wrong, and their own abilities to problem solve.

Now that you have an idea of what consequences are, let's go into a bit more detail on how you can formulate them. While some use the term *consequence* to mean any type of punishment where the discipline meaningfully fits the misdeed, most professionals, myself included, believe there are three basic types of consequences: *natural, logical,* and *applied.*

Natural Consequences

The first, and usually most effective of the three different types of consequences is called *natural consequences.* These occur naturally, without any intervention from you. Your children learn their lesson immediately, from nature, or another child, or in other ways. Here are some examples.

> *Your children don't go to the bathroom before the school field trip; they are uncomfortable during the bus ride and perhaps wet or mess their underwear.*
>
> *Your children don't look where they're going; they trip and fall.*
>
> *Your children touch a hot stove; they experience discomfort or pain and get a blister on their finger.*
>
> *Your children forget their dolls at home; they have nothing to share during show-and-tell time at school.*

Your children speak rudely and sarcastically to another child; the other child punches them in the stomach and stomps on their lunchbox.

The beauty of natural consequences is that you don't have to come in as the heavy or the enforcer. The lessons here are taught by life, by cause-and-effect, and children must either learn the lesson from the experience or possibly face the same consequence once again, somewhere down the line. Keep your eyes open for these natural consequences and appreciate the beauty and perfection of their ability to teach. Prepare your children with knowledge and reasonable warnings of life's natural consequences but, at the same time, observe how marvelously they do teach.

After children have suffered the repercussions of a natural consequence there's no need for you to intervene as a disciplinarian, or remind them of the lesson they should have learned. When your children go outside on a cold day, refusing to wear a coat or sweater, and feel cold and uncomfortable, or forget to bring their snack from home and have to share the teacher's celery and carrot sticks while the other kids are munching on cookies and doughnuts, or are careless with a toy and break it, all you need do ("need" here refers to making sure the lesson is learned. The natural consequence is teaching the lesson. You may have your own need to save your children, which is understandable. Just be sure that you don't "save" them too often, and make them dependent on your interventions.) is comfort them—don't solve the problem for them! Merely comfort them, and be assured that the lesson has been taught as well as it possibly could be by the natural consequence.

You need to be especially careful not to get into the pattern of saving children from these experiences. Of course we save them from physically harmful situations, whenever we can. While we don't want children to be squashed by the realities of life, we also want to beware of becoming "enablers," allowing and assisting our little charges to avoid paying the price for what they do. (Most of us can picture an overprotective adult, hovering over children, shielding them from the world. The question here is, "How much protection is good?")

Logical Consequences

Logical consequences, the next type of consequences, require that both you and your children invest some mental energy and time, discussing and deciding on what the consequences will be for a certain behavior, or certain behaviors. This can happen in either of the following ways.

■ A general discussion, prior to and separate from any specific misbehavior or accidents, may be used to discuss what the logical consequences will be if and when a certain behavior occurs.

or

■ After the misbehavior or accident occurs, you and your children can discuss and agree upon a plan for them to make amends (the logical consequences).

Both approaches can be classified as logical consequences. The "logical" part here is critical. Keeping in mind that adult logic is not the same as child logic, the key is that the consequence seems logical *to the child.* If, during discussions, children come up with a way to make amends for their misdeed, and they can rationalize how the consequence fits the misdeed, it is logical. As a matter of fact, illogical as it may seem to you, children's logical solutions to designing consequences are almost always more effective than parents' logical solutions. Ideally, you'll both see the logic, but the children's understanding is more critical here, for it is they who are supposed to be learning a life lesson. Here are some examples of possible logical consequences that children and adults might agree upon.

Three-year-olds agree to be in bed, with the lights out, by 8:00. They agree that a timer will be started at 8:00 and for every minute they are late—teeth must be brushed, pajamas on, in bed, with lights out—they will lose two minutes of their 30-minute television time the next day.

•••••••••••••••••••••••••••••

Four-year-olds agree with parents that all toys not put away, where they belong, before bedtime, will be placed "in jail" (taken away from them and put into safekeeping). The toy or toys will stay "in jail" for one week, at which time they will be released and become available to be played with again.

. . . .

Eight-year-olds tear their shorts while playing in an off-limits area of the backyard. They sew their own shorts and help build a little barricade to remind them where the off-limits area begins. (No, it's not crazy to have eight-, or even seven- or six-year-olds mend their own shorts in this situation. True, the shorts won't look as good as if you sewed them or bought new ones, but the goal here isn't cute shorts, it's building responsibility and problem solving.)

. . . .

*Six-year-olds lash-out in anger and kick you. They apologize and have to keep their feet "in jail" (in a cardboard box, or on a small carpet area for instance) for five minutes. Sound silly? Not really, not if it was the children's idea. I think we can all see how this might fit into children's logic. Remember, if it's their idea, and if it seems at all reasonable, it will probably be a better consequence (**better** meaning that it will teach the lesson and correct the behavior more assuredly and efficiently than any idea you would have come up with).*

Logical consequences do not have to begin with children; it's better if they do, but the ideas can be yours. They do not have to fit both the children's and your systems of logic, but it's better if they do, and, they usually don't take more than a minute to agree upon, and that's great!

Applied Consequences

Applied consequences may appear from the outside to be exactly the same as logical consequences, but they're different. In applied consequences, the children are not brought into the process of deciding on the consequence. You tell them what the consequence will be, and if you have any doubt that they will understand the logic in your consequence, briefly explain how and why it fits with what they have done. The key difference between the logical and the applied consequence is that children do not participate in the selection of the consequence when it is applied. The key similarity is that applied consequences follow all the previously stated guidelines that define consequences in general. While applied consequences are usually a third choice (first choice is natural—excluding those that injure children; second choice is logical), they are a necessary part of the consequence package, for they allow adults to act quickly and decisively. Examples of applied consequences are

"Quick, get a sponge and clean up that juice before it spreads all over the table."

* * *

"When you speak to me in that tone of voice you don't even need to wait for the answer—I don't respond to orders and threats. The answer will be No, and the answer is No."

* * *

"I'll take that toy. If you two can't play cooperatively with it, then you can't play with it at all."

* * *

"We're leaving. You had plenty of time to brush your hair, and you didn't, so you'll have to do it in the car."

* * *

"You stop that fighting this instant. Now I want you to sit on the couch and talk about this. I'll be back in five minutes and I want to hear what the problem is and how you plan on solving it!"

* * *

"No, Tammy can't spend the night. Remember the last time she did, and the two of you tricked us and stayed up all night playing and watching TV? You could barely function the next day. No, not tonight, Dear."

HOW DO CONSEQUENCES HELP ENCOURAGE POTENTIAL IN CHILDREN?

Consequences are a great alternative to punishment. While the results may come a bit slower, and adults may have to adjust to a new and different system, the benefits are obvious: a system that places more responsibility on children and helps build an internal sense of rules and controls, a system that allows adults to be mutual problem solvers rather than law enforcement officers, and a system that can be continued into later childhood and adolescence, rather than one that distances children from authority figures, and falls apart in a very few years.

For the potential within children to actualize itself, to open up and be shared with others, children must take responsibility. They must decide who they are, what they want, and how hard they are willing to work. Being raised in a system where their rights and responsibilities are respected, where they help make decisions, and where there is order and reason helps children to understand themselves better, to respect adults, to want to become a member of adult society, and to take responsibility for their actions.

Many adults hope and believe that when children turn 13, or 18, or 21, or graduate high school, or graduate college, they will automatically turn into responsible adults, ready and able to take charge of their lives and give it their best. Well, it usually doesn't work that way. The children who do become adults who take charge of their lives and give it their best are usually children whose parents have been guided by these goals for many, many years, parents who have, over a long period of time, given their growing children the opportunity to think for themselves, to learn about themselves, and to take responsibility for their actions.

RECOMMENDATIONS

1. Diminish, or hopefully discard your use of punishment.

2. When your children's behavior leads to a response or reaction from their environment (a natural consequence), only intervene when physical harm may occur and/or after careful consideration. Are you solving their problems for them?

3. Whenever possible discuss logical consequences to misbehavior that might be anticipated, and come to an agreement with your children *prior to* the behavior occurring.

4. Remember, the logic of an adult may not be logical to children, and vice versa. The key in effective logical consequences is that they fit the children's system of logic.

5. When designing applied consequences, make every effort to make them as logical as possible, and explain your logic to the children.

6. Prior to implementing this or any new system, let involved individuals know what you're planning on doing, and why. Don't make them wonder, "What's going on?"

7. If the system described in this chapter is very different from the system you presently use and you start to implement it, you can expect initial resistance and the probable, though temporary, worsening of behavior. Children, like adults, often resist change, even when the change is a positive one.

8. Give it time. Like all other skills in life, it takes time to get really good at something. You'll no doubt stumble and fall—devise unsatisfactory consequences—many times, over many years, but, you'll get better and better at it.

SUMMARY

This chapter has described three different types of consequences that are recommended as alternatives to punishing children. Consequences are recommended as an essential component in encouraging potential in young children because they are rational, help teach children to take responsibility for their behavior, make choices/decisions, and live and grow in harmony with others. While punishments may work more quickly than consequences, their effects are usually short-lived, and the lesson they teach is that might is right and children need to do what they're told, regardless of the logic or lack thereof. Consequences are one of the foundations for building responsible and responsive children.

CHAPTER 4

FOLLOW THEIR LEAD
AND POSITIVE REDIRECTION

INTRODUCTION

This chapter will discuss two important, and closely related ingredients in encouraging your children's potential. The following are these ingredients.

- *Follow their lead*—making an effort, whenever possible, to allow your children to determine the type of play or work they will become involved in and the direction that play or work will take. The foundation of this technique is that children have a natural tendency to become involved in activities that provide them with appropriate practice for developing skills and abilities they are in the process of mastering. If we let them play and work at activities of their own choosing, they will most often involve themselves in productive, growth-producing endeavors.

- *Positive redirection*—carefully and subtly adding to or slightly changing the direction of that play or work when the activity your children are involved in seems to have begun deteriorating or moving in a negative direction, or when you feel a compelling need to change the topic or get more skill or academic practice. This approach is provided as a second choice, to be used cautiously and only occasionally.

Throughout this chapter these two approaches will be blended together. The primary reason for discussing two separate topics simultaneously is that they often occur when playing or working with our children. On the one hand, we probably enjoy watching their excitement and motivation when productively involved in tasks of their own choosing, but, on the other hand, sometimes they become bored with those activities or frustrated and the experience starts to become negative and nonproductive. At other times, we, the parents, have the desire to add ideas to their play or work—perhaps make their activity more challenging or focused on specific skills or academic areas. If we're careful, patient, and flexible, and use these techniques well, we will often be able to do, or have both: to follow their lead and to positively redirect.

THE RELEVANCE OF FOLLOW THEIR LEAD AND POSITIVE REDIRECTION IN THE CONTEXT OF THIS BOOK

Like those techniques discussed in Chapter 2, Encouragement, follow their lead and positive redirection furnish parents with approaches to provide their children with more practice and in-depth exploration and learning. Many parents comment that:

My children won't work with me.

It drives me crazy trying to get them to read anything.

They waste so much time playing the same games, doing the same things, over and over and over again.

They'll do it when they want to, but never when I want them to.

With judicious use of the techniques described in this chapter, parents will make comments like this less often. They will have more understanding and trust in the positive values of their children's self-directed play, be in possession of techniques that, when the occasion arises, may help them slightly change or alter the direction of that play, and, as is the goal in every page of this book, help encourage potential in their children.

When children are allowed to choose the activities they wish to become involved in, and are their own directors, there are usually far fewer concerns about getting them started or interested than when we try to direct them into activities—they're already started and interested! Also, in most cases, when a child has invented a game or activity (such as lining dolls up in a row, stacking blocks, tracing faces in the newspaper, separating a deck of playing cards by suits), they are happy to have someone—someone like you—join in their activity. They like to be the teacher, to teach you their game. When we *join* them, rather than try to *lead* them, the chances are much better that we will share an enjoyable and enriching experience together. (Think about it. Which of the following would tend to evoke a more welcoming response from most children—sitting next to them and joining in with what they're doing, or interrupting their activity and asking them to join you for a lesson on numbers, or letters, or room cleaning techniques?)

Once welcomed into their activity, you have two basic options.

1. Follow their lead. (This is the least threatening approach to them and the one that is most likely to inspire them to interact with you.)

or

2. Subtly attempt to guide or lead the action in certain directions—positive redirection. (This is most appropriate when the activity starts turning in a negative direction, such as boredom, or anger, or frustration, but the technique can also be used cautiously by parents such as myself, who feel that when playing and interacting with their children it's occasionally okay to try and "pump up" or accelerate the level with more challenging vocabulary, movements, or concepts, and perhaps blend in learning objectives and tasks that slightly alter the direction, content, and difficulty of what's going on.) How much and how often we do this determines whether we are subtly redirecting our children or *pushing* them!

HOW AND WHEN TO FOLLOW THEIR LEAD

When children are infants and young toddlers, following their lead comes very naturally. Mimicking or responding to babbling, rolling a ball back and forth to one another, playing peek-a-boo, banging silverware (making music) on the high chair, and picking up and returning objects dropped over the side of the high chair or stroller, again, and again, and again, are all activities we involve ourselves in. They are activities whose developmental relevance few of us would ever question, activities in which children call all the shots and direct all the action, activities that may seem incredibly simple and repetitive, yet, we somehow intuitively know, are necessary for their development.

As toddlers grow more mobile and independent there's usually still a sense that they are finding plenty of things to do to keep themselves productively involved, therefore providing us with limited motivation to influence the direction of their play. We naturally, and correctly, take it for granted that if they are involved in an activity (such as talking in what seem to be non-sense phrases, standing up and falling down, moving toys or objects from one side of the room to the other, building some sort of structure, tearing it down, building it up again, tearing it down, and so on), there is a reason for it, and they need to practice those skills.

Pushing Your Children

As toddlers grow into preschoolers, however, many parents begin thinking that it's time to get down to work, they aren't babies anymore, it's time to start getting them ready for school, that children at this age do not or will not make such appropriate choices in their expenditure of time. These parents start to believe that if they could only get their children to become involved in activities of the parent's choosing, educational and skill-building activities, ABCs/numbers/vocabulary building /pump-up-the-brain/get-'em-ready-for-college type of activities, their children would learn more, or develop in a more positive direction. You may recognize, for example:

The desire to prompt three- or four-year-olds to kick a ball, rather than roll it, accompanied by thoughts such as, "Hey, they can already roll a ball (they've been doing it since they were babies)—why not push them a little into harder stuff!"

Impatience with the large, seemingly sloppy, sometimes off the paper or chalkboard doodlings of four- or five-year-olds, and aggressive and premature attempts to make them draw and write on smaller surfaces with more defined and controlled strokes than come naturally to them.

Frustration that your preschoolers aren't using their memory or language capabilities enough when they refer to all breeds of canines as dogs, which leads to purchasing books and flash cards that illustrate the names and histories of all the various breeds, and setting up tutorial sessions to teach your children more about dogs and to broaden their vocabularies and understanding.

Premature efforts to teach the sounds that letters make to three- to five-year-olds who are just beginning to learn the names of the letters, and to teach counting by twos or fives to children who are just beginning to understand the concept of counting by ones.

As children enter the elementary school years the push-them philosophy accelerates dramatically, often with less than ideal results.

Six- or seven-year-olds—typical, normal, potential-to-be-whatever-they-want-to-be kind of kids—who developmentally (visual perception, auditory discrimination, attention span, motivation) just aren't quite ready to read words and books as they are printed, but find themselves pushed by everyone, day and night, because they are supposed to be starting to read.

Seven- or eight-year-olds who really like and need time to relax, who still enjoy playing with dolls and making up fantasy stories but also happen to be very coordinated and are made to participate after school in gymnastics lessons twice a week, swim team twice a week, and tennis tournaments every Saturday, and rarely given time for free time and relaxation at home.

Five- and six-year-olds who have just learned to write their own names, aren't quite sure of the sounds all the letters make, are just beginning to understand why reading and writing were invented, and rarely use writing to communicate, yet are asked to memorize ten spelling words each week for a written test.

Children who can barely add two single-digit numbers (such as $4 + 3 = \underline{\hspace{1em}}$, $2 + 5 = \underline{\hspace{1em}}$), yet are being asked to learn double-digit addition (such as $24 + 73 = \underline{\hspace{1em}}$, $32 + 45 = \underline{\hspace{1em}}$.)

Underlying parental (and teacher) thoughts and actions such as these may be the belief that children sometimes take the easy route, practicing and playing things that they've already mastered. These grownups believe that if nudged, coaxed, or pushed a little to branch-out into more difficult, higher level activities, development could be accelerated, or supercharged. While this is not a completely wrong philosophy, and an approach that may be justified at times, it is a philosophy/ approach that needs to be carefully analyzed and monitored. When parents become overly involved in these types of thoughts and actions, when they do this more often than their children like or at the expense of depriving them of other activities (developmentally appropriate activities) that they are already involved in, they run a number of risks, such as

- ■ not allowing their children enough practice at activities or skills that are not yet mastered.
- ■ creating in their children a powerless, "I'm not in charge" feeling.
- ■ turning their children off to playing or interacting with them.
- ■ creating unnecessary conflicts or power struggles.

Interrupting Play

Imagine the following scene, one that no doubt has occurred in many thousands of households.

A four- or five- or six-year-old is playing with her dolls, creating a story/dialogue between them. She is completely involved in the fantasy of the situation, and having a thoroughly enjoyable time. The parent comes into the room, observes the child at play, and thinks, "She does this every day, for hours. What have I done wrong? Why does she need so much fantasy play? Do other girls her age do this? This can't be normal! Should I take her to a psychiatrist? Is she going to end up like Aunt Mabel—alone, disturbed, living in a fantasy world? What have I done? I have to stop this! I have to do something. I need to get her involved in math or something. I'm going to end up with a daughter who lives in a fantasy world and can't count to 100." (If you're thinking that this story is one of my self-revelations, you're wrong. This wasn't/isn't me, and it didn't emerge from my own inner thoughts. I have, however, in my role as teacher and professor, been contacted by many parents over the past 25 years who have shared concerns very similar to the one described here.)

The parent then proceeds to interrupt the little girl's play and suggest they count together. The follow-their-lead philosophy recommends that parents be very cautious about actions such as this. While we do want our children to involve themselves in a wide variety of activities, and counting games are appropriate for four- to six-year-olds, dragging children away from healthy, constructive play (which the above described doll activity probably was), in order to introduce a different form of play or academic pursuit, should be approached very cautiously. Why? For the following three reasons:

1. *In this case the child is positively involved in an activity that is building her vocabulary, creativity, and social skills/social perceptions (and, by the way, an abundance of fantasy play, including making up stories, is marvelous in not only four- to six-year-olds, but in seven- to ten-year-olds too).*

> **2.** *The shock and disappointment of being pulled away from the storytelling activity may make it very difficult to reinvolve her in another activity.*
>
> **3.** *Parents would have a far better chance of success in situations such as this if they slowly and subtly entered the fantasy-play situation, and searched for an opportunity to introduce numbers and counting into the natural context of what was going on.*

Whenever possible, parents should avoid interrupting children who are positively involved in work or play. This is especially important regarding creative/artistic activities, where it's most often recommended that parents and teachers watch from a distance. In order to respond to our intrusions, well intended though they may be, children must temporarily leave the creative center of their brain, and, after responding to us, they may not be able to return very easily to the same place or level of creativity. For some this can be quite distressing or upsetting and may lead to a premature end to the project they were so productively involved in. Parents should watch, analyze if and what the value of the work or play might be, and then, if at all possible—if they can think of any value to it—let it continue, uninterrupted.

This doesn't mean that parents should allow children to do anything they want—to watch TV all day and night, or spend three hours a day coloring in coloring books, or finger paint on the walls, or tear pieces of material off the couch to make costumes for their dolls, or open all the cans in the pantry and experiment with a new recipe, or sit at home repeating the same, unchallenging activity over and over again. Parents can and should at times enter into play, or as in some of the examples cited above, parents should feel free to intervene prior to the utter destruction of house and home—and involve themselves with their children. This should occur in these circumstances.

- ■ Adults feel the desire or need either to just be with their children or to teach or show or explain. But, once again, please hold off doing or saying anything to your children while their artistic/creative juices are flowing!

or

- ■ The children's behavior or interest is deteriorating and it's obvious that the activity they're involved in will soon take a negative path or end.

or
■ A teachable moment or golden opportunity arises, and the children seem willing to buy in to the change.

or
■ Once again, we can find no value in what they are doing and/or we fear the end of civilization as we know it. (Keep in mind that even though you find it hard to see value in their activity, there probably is some. Some form of learning or practice is probably taking place.)

When any of these situations occur, go for it! Move slowly, cautiously, and with sensitivity but, by all means, go for it! If the little guy or gal remains bright-eyed and open, go ahead and be the teacher, go ahead and work on those letters or numbers or concepts. Watch your children carefully, and make sure that their interest and involvement are still there but let the teacher/learning guide in you loose. If and when they begin struggling against your direction, then it's time to back off. And remember, it's far better to end most activities one minute before boredom sets in rather than one minute after. Human beings tend to associate feelings with activities, and the feelings that tend to stick the best in children's minds are those experienced near the end of an activity. So end with fun and excitement, not boredom and friction.

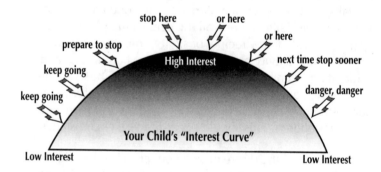

How to Join in Children's Play

You may be wondering, "If I do want to join my children in play, how do I go about it?" The first step is body proximity—move in closer. Your children will usually let you know if your approach is welcome. "Go away; Mommy," "Daddy, you be the dog and I'll be the cat," "Look what I'm doing," "Play with me" are some pretty clear messages. If not invited, or if a clear sign does not emerge, the next step is to move in even closer. Once you're near your children, physically position yourself to join in; for instance sit on the floor, find a place near them at the table, or pick up one of the marbles or dolls they're playing with. The idea is to be asked to join and be told your role. That process is slower than jumping right in, but the chances of success are greatly heightened by patience. If these first two ideas—moving in closer and positioning yourself to join in—don't lead to an invitation, other ploys may be tried.

1. Positively comment on the play or describe what you see going on. Beware of questioning children in this situation. Questioning is a technique that is vastly overrated; it usually doesn't work as well and it doesn't engage children as much as the other techniques described here.

2. Ask if you can join in.

3. Begin to nonverbally participate by laughing, smiling, singing along, creating a background for the scene.

POSITIVE REDIRECTION TECHNIQUES

Once in, and your children are playing with you, enjoy yourself and witness their abundant creativity and intelligence. Make every effort to go with their flow, but if you feel a need, you may try to incorporate new and different aspects into the play (positive redirection). In the case of the little girl playing dolls, and the parent wanting math and counting, the parent might seize upon an opportunity such as the following.

Child: Okay, let's feed the baby now. Come on, Mommy, you hold her like this, and give her the food like this.

Parent: Yes, she has to eat her peas so she'll be strong. She needs lots and lots of peas.

Child: Yes, lots of peas. Let's feed her together. Come on. You hold her and I'll feed her.

Parent: Okay. Let's give her 30 peas—one, two, three, four, five (child and parent count together).

Deceptive though this technique may seem to you, your children will probably regard it as an appropriate addition to their fantasy, and gladly count along. They will almost certainly still feel that they are leading the action and are in charge, and will therefore be much more likely to participate in the counting activity.

Let's look at another example of positive redirection.

> *A four- to eight-year-old is running around the basement, pretending to shoot, stab, cut, slug, chop, maim, and utterly destroy every form of imaginary life he or she comes into contact with.*

The parent who wishes to change the direction of this child's play may try to stop the fantasy and attempt to introduce another activity (an approach that I've already advised against) or try to enter the child's play and more slowly and unobtrusively change the direction (positive redirection). This approach may, on a good day, result in a dialogue like the one that follows.

Child: Let's blow them up. Here, let's use these pennies and pretend they're bombs and we'll blow up all those soldiers over there. We'll throw the pennies, I mean bombs, and knock them over and kill them.

Parent: Wait, give me a minute to talk to the big one over there (points to a figure larger than the others). Maybe we can work something out without wasting all our bombs—we may need them later! There may be another attack and then we'll be out of bombs.

Child: Come on, let's kill them, blow them up. I don't want to talk to them— they'll trick us and kill us. Let's blast 'em.

Parent: We can't. Wait. Hold it. He's holding up a white flag. (Parent takes out a piece of tissue and waves it close to the ground.) He wants to talk to us. Look, he's coming this way. (Parent moves figure closer to child.)

Child: Okay, I'll talk to him, but if he tries anything you shoot him, cut him up, tear him to bits. Okay? Shoot 'em all. Cover me now, and remember, bomb 'em all if they try anything.

Parent: Okay, Captain. Whatever you say. Good luck.

Child: (Enters a dialogue with the enemy, a dialogue that the parent assists with, one that models negotiation and conflict resolution skills that this child is in great need of developing. The parent might even take over the voice of the enemy soldier and directly negotiate with the child.)

While this technique won't always work (the child may "blow them up" despite your pleas) and it may seem slow and cumbersome, it *may* work, and if it does, this child will have one more option to consider the next time he or she is involved in fantasy play, or even in a real-life situation with other children, perhaps while playing outside or on the school playground.

Follow their lead is a technique that allows parents to enter their children's play, connect with them in a fun and involving way, and, when the opportunity arises, positively redirect (extend or enrich) the quality of the play, or perhaps move it in new directions.

RECOMMENDATIONS

1. Watch and listen to your children at play and work, and consider the positive value—what they are learning—and why the activity is important to and for them.

2. Make every effort not to disturb children who are actively and productively involved in an activity; one word may break their flow and end what was a valuable and enriching experience.

3. If you do decide to enter their play, move in slowly. Show interest and wait to be asked to join.

4. If you are not asked to join in, and you still wish to do so, begin by using nonverbal signs of approval; limit comments to a minimum and make them positive.

5. Beware of asking questions. Many children do not respond as well to questions, (which may stifle their interactions or limit their verbalizations), as they do to the other techniques described here.

6. Provide as rich and varied an educational environment (open spaces, balls, toys, games, writing and reading materials) as possible.

7. Beware of being too pushy, of rushing children into experiences they aren't ready for. Be patient.

8. When you do intervene in your children's play or work, make every effort to do it subtly, slowly, and with sensitivity. Start where they are and branch off from there.

SUMMARY

One of the best ways to form or enhance a relationship with another individual is through shared interests and activities. When we see our children actively, excitedly, and productively engaged in play or work, we are provided with an excellent opportunity to join them (to follow their lead) and share the joy and excitement of their curiosity, intelligence, creativity, and self-expression. Once we are accepted as a part of their activity, it is usually enough to simply interact with them, without any specific goals or outcomes in mind; our being together will provide benefit to both them and us. If, however, we wish to introduce new elements into their play or work (positive redirection), we should do so subtly, slowly, and in a positive way, constantly monitoring their interest level and endeavoring to maintain their excitement and motivation.

CHAPTER 5

EMERGING SKILLS

INTRODUCTION

The emerging skills philosophy holds that all, or most, skills or abilities begin their development at birth (if not before) and then mature and are refined throughout childhood and adult life. According to this philosophy, the early foundations of reading, logical-mathematic understanding, social skills, coordination, and all other areas of human development are present in newborns, at which time the groundwork for how far individuals will reach or achieve begins its formation.

> ## THE RELEVANCE OF EMERGING SKILLS IN THE CONTEXT OF THIS BOOK
>
> *If we are to truly encourage potential in children, the sooner we start the better. The earlier we identify and nurture children's strengths, as well as paying attention to and remediating areas of development that may emerge slowly, the better. This chapter will describe how parents can help their children develop solid foundations for later more academic and formal instruction and practice in many developmental areas.*

Before going into detail on the specific steps or stages in various emerging skills, and how parents can provide enriching environments to help their children in these areas, let's look at a few brief examples of the process.

> *Six-month-olds, grasping for bottles, pacifiers, their feet, and everything around them are practicing skills that need to be mastered before they can color with crayons (at the age of two years), put puzzles together (when they are three and four), pick up dirty laundry and toys and clean up their rooms (when they are seven and eight) or, as adults, gather materials and handle the cooking utensils required to make a casserole.*

A newborn rocking in Daddy's lap as he sings lullabies to her and a two-year-old sitting quietly as Mommy reads a storybook to him are both developing skills, practicing, preparing themselves, if you will, for sitting, listening, and taking notes in a high school history class, sitting in a large examination hall and listening to the directions for the Law School Admissions Test or Graduate Records Exam and attending a Shakespearean play.

Six-year-olds who enjoy creating towers, forts, and castles out of building blocks, playing counting games, and seeing if there are more white cars or red cars traveling on the highway, are involving themselves in very appropriate activities that will help them to someday perform better in algebra and geometry classes, and perhaps lead them to careers in engineering, or architecture, or mathematics.

Eight-year-olds who love to be with other children, help friends solve problems and make decisions, and organize games and activities, may well be practicing and experimenting with skills that could lead to a college degree in psychology, or recreation, or social work, or counseling, that may develop into careers as psychotherapists, or recreation directors, or social workers, or counselors.

The idea here is that learning begins very early in life. Early childhood, childhood, adolescence, young adulthood, and adulthood are not separate journeys, but part of the same journey. One doesn't finish or complete a certain level of understanding, or developmental skills, and then move on to the next level; all levels, all learning is connected. We human beings, without years of practice, attention to detail, motivation, and an environment that helps us from an early age, almost certainly cannot and will not

- ■ wake up on our eleventh birthday with great hand-eye coordination and drawing abilities.
- ■ turn from uninterested, short attention span, three-years-behind-grade-level tenth graders, to Stanford University literature majors.

■ develop great interest or ability in logical-mathematical thinking after a childhood in which this area of the brain has received little attention or stimulation.

■ become socially aware leaders or helping professionals, after years of being a loner, not showing concern for others, and not being reinforced for our efforts at helping others.

STARTING EARLY

T he following sections will discuss a number of developmental areas in which the emerging skills philosophy or approach is of critical importance. In these sections parents will learn to identify how sequential stages of skills emerge, and how to set up environments that encourage children to use these skills and maximize their potential in

■ sensory awareness.
■ coordination/movement/dance/sports.
■ language/reading/writing.
■ logical-mathematical thinking/science.
■ the arts.
■ social/psychological skills.
■ other areas that are of specific interest or in which your children demonstrate particular aptitudes.

SENSORY AWARENESS

T he vast majority of children learn to use their senses and integrate various types of stimulation with little or no difficulty. From gustatory (mouth sensations and taste), to olfactory (smells), to tactile awareness (touch and feelings through the skin), to kinesthetic (movement and balance), to auditory (hearing) and visual (seeing), stimuli begin bombarding the growing fetus, and continue into infancy and throughout life. Children must not only learn to perceive these senses—to experience them—but they must also learn to interrelate them (for instance, milk looks white and liquidy, tastes rich and creamy, smells deep and earthy; fire feels warm or hot or burning hot, looks bright and flickering, is of varied colors, and sounds crackling or blowing; Christmas smells fresh, green, earthy, and cinnamony, tastes sweet and yummy, looks green, red, and white, feels cold and warm and exciting), and to remember each sensation and store that memory for future use.

We parents tend to take for granted that our children will learn to use all their senses well, integrate and coordinate them together, and remember and use the experience and knowledge gained from them. We tend to think that this process will occur naturally, without requiring any of our attention or intervention. This may be so for most children, most of the time, but for some it is not how things work. For example:

Children with significant sensory impairments, such as those who are deaf or blind, must be taught to use what little hearing or vision they may have, and must learn to take greater advantage of their intact senses, use those senses in ways that others, those without sensory impairments, may not need to (for instance, the blind need to listen more carefully to sounds that are approaching them, for they cannot count on their vision to warn them of impending danger; the deaf need to be more observant of nonverbal communications than do individuals who can hear, for those communications may help interpret meaning when verbal messages aren't completely communicated).

Children who are born tactually defensive (not caring for or liking being touched) must be taught to tolerate some touching and being touched, to order their environment so that they are less overwhelmed by this sensory feedback, and to deal with the negative feelings it may arouse in them.

Children with sensory integration difficulties—deficits in understanding and properly using information from their senses (including many children and adults with learning disabilities, attention-deficit/hyperactivity disorders, and mental retardation/developmental disabilities)—are greatly benefited by occupational and/or physical therapy to assist them in preparing themselves for learning and functioning in life (see Chapter 11, Groups at Risk of Not Realizing Their Potential).

Children with exceptional potential in appreciating and/or utilizing different sensory modalities require more and enriched experiences in order to make the most of their innate abilities (for example young painters may require richer visual environments, young chefs richer gustatory and olfactory environments, and young athletes richer and more challenging kinesthetic environments).

How can we do this? How can we be sure that we're providing our children with rich experiences that will help them learn from their senses, develop possible deficit areas, and make the most of their potential? The answer, like the answer for each of the following sections of this chapter, is to provide your children with rich and varied environments, and make every effort to bring their attention to experiencing and utilizing their senses, and then discuss with them their perceptions. For example:

Parent bathing six-month-old: "Let's scrub your back with this washcloth. Now that feels good, doesn't it? Not too rough, I hope. How do you like it, Sweetie—soft, like this, or a little harder, like this? Let's make some circles on your back, around and around and around. Now, let's go up and down, up and down, up and down. We'll do your face, oh so gently, and your little fingers, one, two, three, four..."

Parent sitting in the yard with three-year-olds: "Smell this rose, it sure has a strong smell, doesn't it? How does it smell to you? Does this remind you of any smells you've smelled before? Let's go smell all the flowers and talk about how they smell. We'll pick our favorites! I know, let's close our eyes and smell different flowers and guess their colors."

Parent to five-year-olds: "I've got a good game—let's see how many different shades of green we can find in this big box of crayons and then we'll line them up from lighter to darker. Let's put the lighter ones over here and the darker ones over there. If we find two that are the same we can just put them together. Maybe we can even think of good names, funny names, for the different colors."

Parent to seven-year-olds: "Okay, close your eyes and I'm going to put things in your hands and you have to describe them and tell what you think they are. First tell me how they feel, say everything you can think of to tell about how they feel and then guess what it is. Want to play? Great! We could take turns. Do you want to go first, or me?"

Parent to eight-year-olds: "Hey, why don't we work on that assignment your teacher gave you? We can make up some haiku poems about things we find outside. We can write about how they look and sound and smell and feel. The assignment said you had to write two poems and each one had to include how many adjectives, six? This will be fun!"

The idea here is to motivate our children to use their senses in fun and varied ways, to heighten their awareness and appreciation of stimuli that are naturally and constantly entering their consciousness, to teach them, if and when the need arises, to get the most out of their sensory channels that may in some way be impaired, and to actualize their potential for appreciating and using channels that may otherwise not be appreciated or used as well as they might.

COORDINATION/MOVEMENT/DANCE/SPORTS

Many years ago I worked with a four-year-old who was an overall good athlete but absolutely incredible at kicking a soccer ball and bouncing the ball from his head to his feet to his knees to his shoulders and back and forth. I mentioned this to his parents, who were both soccer enthusiasts, and they were very pleased but also very surprised. They hadn't spent much time playing ball games or outdoor sports-type activities with their son, and had never really noticed that he was different—more advanced—from other children his age. We discussed it, and they decided to start playing more sports-type activities with him, enroll him in a soccer league, and sign him up for soccer camp that coming summer. Now for the question: Were that boy's chances of actualizing his sports/soccer potential the same, greater, or less after my discussion with his parents? I trust you have reached the same conclusion I reached. I think the chances were greater. I have to believe that the extra attention, time, caring, and instruction that my comments helped stimulate brought that young boy to a more advanced level than had I not said anything.

Ever since that experience with the young soccer player, one of my favorite activities or hobbies in life—sort of a mission—has been to keep my eyes and ears wide open, looking for individuals who may possess significant amounts of potential, in any area, and share my observations with that person and others who may be involved in that person's life. I can't tell you how many times I have shared my observations and found that no one before had ever thought or mentioned that a significant area of potential might exist. Children, as well as their parents, very often don't realize how good they are in something, how great their potential is, or what can or might be done to develop that potential. The more I do this the more I think it's important to look for these abilities in everyone and share our observations. Sometimes I sort of feel like Cupid, but instead of using arrows to help people fall in love, I'm using words and observations, to motivate children and their parents to appreciate what they have and use it more fully. I welcome you to play this game yourself—search for potential and share your observations! Another example:

> *There are two eight-year-old girls with identical body types and genetic makeups/potential in the area of grace and movement coordination. At the age of eight one is enrolled in ballet classes, which she enjoys and attends twice a week for the next ten years, while the other never attends any dance classes or receives any type of outside encouragement in this area.*

Which girl will probably be more graceful at the age of 18? Which girl has been provided with a giant head start toward either a career or a lifelong hobby/interest area? You know which one, don't you? (If you had any difficulty with this question, and could not identify the girl who received extra instruction as the one most likely to reach higher levels of achievement, then I recommend you return to page one of this book and start again.)

We can't make our children become athletes or dancers, but we can set up environments that encourage development in these areas and others. The first level is our becoming aware of our children's abilities/areas of potential. Our awareness, of and by itself, sets a stage for providing opportunities to enhance development. We also want to let our children know what we see and think regarding their potential. This not only helps to encourage them—knowing that we perceive them as being, having, or possessing a special "gift" or ability—but also creates a curiosity in them. It heightens the chances that they will begin looking for signs of this potential themselves, which may help motivate them to work on themselves and improve.

What you may be thinking is, "Okay, but I can't do it all. I can't be watching every move my children make, looking for every sign of potential, enrolling them in ten different classes; and having them participate in two extracurricular activities, every day." That's true, but you can

■ have lots of open areas where infants and toddlers can safely scoot, roll, crawl, stand, fall, and walk around, and only use devices that restrict their movement (high chairs, cribs, walkers) when absolutely necessary.

■ provide toddlers and preschoolers with balls to bounce, kick, and throw, safe areas in which to run, fall, roll, tumble, and ride trikes, bikes, and scooters.

■ build a play structure in the yard, or take your preschoolers and young children to the park, where they can swing, slide, and climb.

■ allow and encourage your children, regardless of their ages, to feel the rhythms of music, to move their bodies, to dance.

■ look for areas of development that are challenging to or frustrating your children. Search for enticing and fun ways for them to improve in those areas so that they will not be handicapped by any deficits in skills or attitudes (for instance "I can't climb," "I'm not a good dancer," "I don't like to play catch—I'm no good at it").

■ help your children discover ways to enjoy experiencing their bodies and sports and activities in areas in which they have more potential for enjoyment and excellence (such as swimming, ballet, soccer, or gymnastics). Provide extra encouragement in those areas and search for resources to help them use and improve in those skills, as in the following ways.

  • access to a pool for children who love to swim

  • music and an open space in your house and perhaps dance lessons for children who get joy from expressing themselves through movement

  • a ball, a field, and partners/friends or a team for children who like soccer

  • an open space with a padded floor and gymnastics lessons for children who enjoy rolling and flipping and jumping

Most children don't require advanced training or sophisticated mentors during the first few years of life, although this can be very beneficial for children with exceptional levels of potential (this topic will be discussed further in Chapter 11). Most kids just need the opportunity to use what they've got. We're the ones whose job it is to provide them with those opportunities.

LANGUAGE/READING/WRITING

Have you ever wondered why it is that children who are surrounded by adults who speak clearly and properly (using standard rules of grammar, syntax, and pragmatics), with minimal use of profanity, tend to mature into individuals who speak clearly and properly, with minimal use of profanity?

Why is it that children who are brought up in homes where language is used both as a tool to communicate as well as a vehicle for creative expression or an art form meant to be investigated, played with, practiced, and perfected, develop richer, more varied, and more entertaining ways to use language, to play with thoughts and words, and as a vehicle for creative expression?

Do those children who are raised in homes with lots of books and other printed material, where adults read a lot, have a greater likelihood of doing well in school and becoming better readers?

If they are encouraged and required to write more frequently, for a variety of purposes, do they learn to express themselves more freely, joyously, and competently through their writing?

I think you sense where this is leading. While our potential may vary in these areas, experiences are far more important in learning to master the skills of oral language, reading, and writing. More specifically, the first few years of most children's lives determine, to a large extent, how they communicate with language, both orally and in written form. Therefore, be aware of the following points.

1. If you want your children to someday competently understand and speak your native language, then, beginning at birth or as soon after as possible, speak to them in sentences, with clear pronunciation, differing sentence structures, and a varied vocabulary. (Baby talk won't hurt children, if used in reasonable doses, but it is not recommended as an approach to teaching young children to talk.)

2. Read to your babies. Read to your toddlers. Read to your preschoolers. And, read to your school-age children. Read all types of books, discuss them, and have them "read" to

you. With young children this will probably first take the form of made-up stories about the books, and will later become memorized recitations of stories you've read to them.

3. Write to your children, of all ages, and accept their early squiggles as writing. Have them "read" their notes to you. Leave mail for one another around the house, and encourage them to "write" (even if it's just varied marks and shapes that only they can read) to friends, to their teachers, to Grandma Shirley, and to Uncle Fred.

Just do it! That's the key. If you think that seventh grade grammar class is where your children are going to someday learn to speak clearly and properly, forget it! The first words they hear from you are their first lesson, and you're the primary teacher for their English Grammar and Pronunciation I and II and III and IV courses. Don't think for a moment that your five-, six-, or seven-year-olds are going to *start* to learn to read in kindergarten or first grade—they *started* to learn to read the first time you read a book to them. And, if you're hoping that your son or daughter will learn to become a writer, or start really writing, in a freshman composition class, once they start their university training, you've seriously underestimated the critical importance of the little zeros they were drawing in their mashed potatoes and gravy when they were two; the seemingly meaningless string of As, Bs, and Cs they put together underneath their crayon drawings when they were four, and the error-riddled, simplistic letters they begged you to mail to friends and family when they were seven and eight.

Just do it! Talk to them, listen to them, read to them, have them read to you, write them letters and notes, and have them "write" to you and other loved ones—that's how they learn to do it. With a good start, with four or five or six years at home, with you, doing all of these things, your children's foundations for later accomplishments in oral and written language will be firmly established.

LOGICAL-MATHEMATICAL THINKING/SCIENCE

B ased on the facts that you selected this book to read, you've stayed with it to this point, and you have just read the previous sections on Sensory Awareness, Coordination/Movement/Dance/Sports, and Language/Reading/Writing, my guess is that you can anticipate the basic message of this section. Let's try an experiment. Before reading any further, picture in your mind what you think is going to be recommended in the following paragraphs. In what ways are logical and mathematical thinking and science "emerging" in young children? How might you set up environments that encourage your children to use these skills and maximize their potential? Please close your eyes and think for a minute before reading further.

Well done! My guess is that you just thought of some very relevant and important points. If you did, you can now move to the next paragraph and read on. If you didn't—my years of teaching experience have taught me that students (for the moment that group includes you) don't always follow directions—then once again I ask you to please *think.*

Okay, you are now in possession of a number of ideas about how mathematical thinking and science are emerging in young children, and also how one might set up environments that encourage children to use these skills and maximize their potential. However, I feel compelled to add some more information to what are certainly wonderful ideas that you have already come up with. It's true that you will probably not remember most of the details in the following paragraphs, but please bear with me; I did spend years investigating this topic and I want to impress you with my knowledge, even if it is just for a brief moment.

Early Stages

The earliest stages would be hard to guess, unless you've had some training in child development. In math one of many early steps is gaining an understanding of *object permanence*—that it exists, even if it hides under the blanket or goes into another room. In science one early stage would be *curiosity,* or the desire to experience, experiment, and understand. From these and other points young children move to hundreds of other areas of awareness and understanding, including the understanding of concepts such as *the same, bigger and smaller, alike and different, first, second, third…, above and below, more and less,* and *before and after.* Somewhere along the way children learn that numbers represent something—something like *how many*—and that actions have results (for instance, push the ball and it moves, drop the bottle on the ground and it falls and goes "bang," plant a seed and a flower grows, blow and the candle goes out). Young mathematicians and scientists must learn to separate and categorize all the information their brains assimilate and store the information for further use. All in all, it's a very exciting, rapidly developing, and complex but natural process.

Supporting Children's Development

Let's look at some examples of logical, mathematical, and scientific intelligence in children, and identify ways in which we naturally support our children's development and also extra ingredients parents can add to encourage even higher levels of understanding and achievement.

To someday understand Einstein's Theory of Relativity, young scientists and mathematicians must first learn to become aware of their environments. Comparing, contrasting, counting, categorizing, and a thousand other naturally occurring activities of human brains are parts of this awareness. Environments that provide these experiences are aiding in the development of logical-mathematical and scientific understanding. Junior scientist kits, microscopes, calculators, and computers with math and science programs, are all great additions that can encourage children in these fields and help them actualize their potential, but they aren't absolutely necessary for typical children.

In order for a seventh grader to successfully solve the following problem: "If the length of a room is 12 feet and the width is 10 feet, how much will it cost to lay new carpet in the room if the padding + carpet + installation is $8.75/square yard?" that student must have learned, years before, that numbers represent something (such as size, quantity, and so on), that 1 + 1 = 2, and that there are nine square feet in one square yard. Parents who supply their children with blocks, beads, counting chips, sand and water and measuring utensils are helping them prepare for problems like this, problems that will confront them later in their schooling and life. It would benefit most children to also have experience at home working with a tape measure, to practice designing shapes and pictures on paper, and actually becoming involved in projects that required some or all of the understanding and computation skills required in the above problem. These activities, however, aren't absolutely necessary in order for a seventh grader to solve the problem.

. . . .

No student has ever passed high school chemistry or algebra without learning many years before that certain processes require that a specific sequence or order of events be followed. A kindergartner who is learning to put three or four picture or cartoon squares in order, memorizing the days of the week and months of the year, following their daily schedule on the activity board that hangs above the chalkboard, and preparing a snack following the numbered cards in the kindergarten cookbook, is practicing skills that must be mastered before other learning, learning that is required to succeed in those high school courses, can take place. Basic everyday household items, games, and toys, mixed with a little bit of parental organizing and ingenuity, is usually enough to stimulate these emerging skills. Children who need more—those who demonstrate a real interest or aptitude in these areas—should be provided with more (doing experiments at home, charting and graphing different physical phenomenon, computer simulations, and additional instruction/tutoring).

THE ARTS

T his and the following sections should not require nearly as much detail as the beginning parts of this chapter—you've got the basic theory of how skills emerge and develop throughout childhood and life. The challenge now is applying that basic knowledge or understanding to different areas, and using that understanding to provide an environment that will enhance your children's development.

While some children may be born to be fabulous artists or musicians, for most, the expression of creativity and artistic talent is more a product of life experiences and motivation than genetics. It's important for parents to provide children with materials such as paper, pencils, crayons, markers, water colors, Play-Doh, clay, drums, rhythm sticks, and tambourines, to entice them to express themselves in various ways, to model for them their own enjoyment and fulfillment when involved in creative/artistic endeavors, to help them experience the joy of creating sights and sounds of beauty, and to encourage them to enjoy both the process of creating art and the product—completing projects.

It's very difficult to make a living as a full-time artist (just ask most artists!), but everyone can have their lives enhanced through the infusion of more art and creativity in everything they do.

Most children aren't interested in devoting themselves to a musical instrument, but all children benefit from being exposed to music, encouraged to sing and feel rhythms, and supplied with necessary materials and lessons if and when an interest emerges.

SOCIAL/PSYCHOLOGICAL SKILLS

I t goes without saying that all children need to be assisted or nurtured in feeling good about who they are, need reinforcing experiences to help them develop positive self concepts, and need to learn to get along with others.

Most psychologists believe that by the age of five or six (some say as early as two or three), children have developed self-images about who they are, what they like and dislike, and their abilities and deficiencies, as well as definite styles or approaches to dealing with other people. The six-year-old whiner has a pretty good likelihood of becoming the 30-year-old whiner; the five-year-old I-can-do-anything go-getter is well on her way to emerging as a 40-year-old I-can-do-anything go-getter; the three-year-old entertainer/joke teller/life of the party/give-me-an-audience-and-I'll-entertain-them kind of kid is very probably going to spread joy and laughter for many decades; and the four-year-old shy, quiet, loner will probably need some significant interventions or face an adult life as a shy, quiet, loner.

While these tendencies to act or be a certain way seem to emerge quite early in life, they are by no means completely predetermined, unalterable, or inflexible. We aren't powerless to change or transform what seem to be early predispositions or personality traits. The vast majority of children, with the assistance of caring adults, can take positive steps to enhance their social and psychological functioning. We don't have to be or become someone or something just because we seemed to have early tendencies in that direction. Experience is the key. Providing children with the right experiences—experiences that lead to feelings of success, experiences that teach caring for others, experiences that teach values. In other words,

> *If your children want to be more socially accepted, or you wish them to be more socially accepted, set up situations in which this will happen (for instance, begin by encouraging them to play with one, easy-to-get-along with child, and experience success. Build slowly on successes. Over time, move to playing with other children, and more children, in a variety of environments).*
>
> •••••••••••••••••••••••••••••
>
> *If your children, at an early age, seem to be developing tendencies to be fearful or nervous, set up situations (such as counseling, breathing exercises, visualizations, meditations) where they can learn to practice relaxation. Also, investigate the types of experiences or situations that make them the most nervous or fearful and avoid overtaxing them in those types of environments. Attempt to expose them to their fears in small doses, with lots of support, so they can learn to deal with them (positive experiences tend to lead to more positive feelings).*

If your children crave the attention of others, and are developing inappropriate attention-seeking habits to attract that attention, help them discover skills, abilities, and techniques within themselves that can get them attention, but in more positive ways (such as singing, telling jokes, achievement in sports or academics).

If your children seem to crave power and getting their own way, and are developing inappropriate power-seeking types of behaviors—such as being bossy or a bully, always having to be in charge, becoming oppositional or defiant when they don't get their way—set up situations where they can feel powerful and in charge without attempting to dominate others. Guide them into karate or debate/forensics lessons, involve them in the scouts and the pursuit of badges and awards, get them into training dogs… whatever, anything you or they can think of that will help meet their needs for power.

If not dealt with, bad habits tend to get worse, and more ingrained; personality flaws tend to intensify and become more and more dominating; social inadequacies tend to move individuals further and further from healthy interpersonal/social relationships.

Don't wait too long. Don't think that the annoying or disturbing tendencies, attitudes, or social behavior of your children are only temporary (although they may be, as in the cases of the terrible twos and the fearful, foul-mouthed fours).

On the brighter side, enjoy and take advantage of any special aptitudes (potential) your children seem to have in these areas. Some children are born with significant potential in interpersonal (between people) and intrapersonal (understanding self) skills. These children can benefit tremendously from activities such as

- having the opportunity to play and work with a wide variety of different children, in a variety of settings.
- joining different groups and participating in different types of social events (such as afterschool activities, summer camps, play groups, scouts, becoming an actor/actress camps and classes).
- spending time and being involved with a wider age range of children, both younger and older than themselves.
- sharing their feelings with others.
- reading and having stories read to them about people dealing with emotions and feelings and interacting well with one another.
- keeping a journal about their lives and thoughts.

For some children, early experiences such as these can help them gain even greater levels of awareness and understanding of themselves and others and may help lead them into exciting and rewarding careers in teaching, social work, writing, counseling, psychology, politics, recreation, or any field in which emotions, sensitivity, or interpersonal skills are required.

OTHER AREAS

I t's now *your* turn to come up with the ideas. Think of your children: What skills and abilities do you see emerging in them? In what areas have they revealed particular aptitudes or interests? In what, if any, areas do you anticipate they will face challenges or hurdles to achievement? What are you doing to help them actualize their potential? What else could you do? A sample chart is filled out and discussed on the next page. Read it. Think about it. Then fill out the chart on page 97 as it relates to your children.

Judy's **Personal Chart**

Your child's name

	Low Potential	Average Potential	Great Potential
Artistic Ability	☐	☐	☑
Artistic Appreciation	☐	☐	☑
Musical Ability	☐	☑	☐
Musical Appreciation	☑	☐	☐
Dance	☐	☑	☐
Sports	☐	☑	☐
Language	☐	☑	☐
Creativity	☐	☐	☑
Math	☐	☑	☐
Science	☐	☑	☐
Interpersonal (Social)	☐	☑	☐
Intrapersonal (Self understanding)	☐	☑	☐
Sense of Humor	☐	☑	☐
stubborn Other	☐	☐	☑
outgoing Other	☑	☐	☐
loving Other	☐	☐	☑

Please fill in the following blanks. Select areas/categories from the above chart in which your child demonstrates the greatest and lowest amounts of potential.

	Area	What are you doing?	What have you thought of doing?
1.	art (high)	materials at home; encouragement; parents model art pursuits	summer class and art camp; set up art area at home
2.	music appre. (low)	play good music at home; take to concerts; encourage when possible	give her stereo and music of her choice; talk to school music teacher
3.	outgoing (very shy)	ask her to have friends over	see a counselor; join play group; spend more time with cousins
4.			
5.			
6.			

Personal Chart

_____
Your child's name

	Low Potential	Average Potential	Great Potential
Artistic Ability	☐	☐	☐
Artistic Appreciation	☐	☐	☐
Musical Ability	☐	☐	☐
Musical Appreciation	☐	☐	☐
Dance	☐	☐	☐
Sports	☐	☐	☐
Language	☐	☐	☐
Creativity	☐	☐	☐
Math	☐	☐	☐
Science	☐	☐	☐
Interpersonal (Social)	☐	☐	☐
Intrapersonal (Self understanding)	☐	☐	☐
Sense of Humor	☐	☐	☐
Other	☐	☐	☐
Other	☐	☐	☐
Other	☐	☐	☐

Please fill in the following blanks. Select areas/categories from the above chart in which your child demonstrates the greatest and lowest amounts of potential.

	Area	What are you doing?	What have you thought of doing?
1.	_____	_____	_____
2.	_____	_____	_____
3.	_____	_____	_____
4.	_____	_____	_____
5.	_____	_____	_____
6.	_____	_____	_____

Compared to other children, your children may not have any incredible gifts or talents or areas of fantastic potential but, compared to themselves, they no doubt have areas of greater ability or potential. Think about it, investigate, and then share your insights with your children. Discuss what you might do, together, to help them be the most they can be.

Don't wait to do this. As this chapter has explained, your six-month-old and your two-year-old and your seven-year-old are all sending signals, providing you with information about who they are, and how they are developing. Every child, at every age, is working on every skill, ability, and area of interest that they will ever possess. Without being too pushy, without turning your children into little achievement machines, is there more that you might be doing to encourage them?

RECOMMENDATIONS

1. Provide your children with a varied, rich, and stimulating environment, beginning at birth or before.

2. Keep in mind that every aspect of who infants will someday be begins development at or before birth. A *whole* infant, one who is provided with and takes advantage of opportunities to learn and grow in all areas, tends to become a *whole* child, who will, if the environment is rich and balanced, eventually emerge as a *whole* adult.

3. Make an effort to identify developmental areas of particular strength, as well as areas that may challenge your children, and provide extra opportunities to explore and learn in these areas.

4. For most children, in most areas of development, common, everyday materials, mixed with parental attention and involvement, are enough to meet their needs, and stimulate development.

5. In some cases (in particular, children with exceptional potential and children with possible disabilities), special materials and specific types of instruction may be necessary.

SUMMARY

All, or most, skills and abilities begin their development at birth, if not before, and then mature and are refined throughout childhood and adult life. The early foundations of reading, logical-mathematical understanding, social skills, coordination, and all other areas of human development, are present in the newborn. It is of utmost importance that parents be aware of this and begin as early as possible to establish a rich and varied environment for their children, an environment where children can experience their senses, explore with their bodies, use the many and varied parts of their intellect, take creative chances, and learn about themselves and how they fit in the world of people.

Besides providing this rich environment, parents also need to pay special attention to those developmental areas that seem to stand out from other areas (both personal strengths and potential challenges, or areas of possible disability). When these occur, parents need to do more than provide a standard, rich environment; they need to go beyond—to seek out other resources so that their children can make the most of what they have.

CHAPTER 6

MODELING

INTRODUCTION

C hildren have a tendency to observe significant people in their lives, most notably parents, and adopt attitudes, behavior, and characteristics similar to those individuals. Sometimes consciously and sometimes subconsciously, they try to behave and be like those people. This process is called *modeling*.

As parents, we hope that our children will only model on *some* of our attitudes and behaviors, the ones we regard as good. Keeping in mind that our children can and do often model on both our admirable traits (respecting and loving our parents, helping others, working hard to keep our family running efficiently, good posture, brushing our teeth before bed, listening while being spoken to, and so on), as well as our less desirable traits (not cleaning up after ourselves, being late for appointments, eating too fast, speaking negatively about people behind their backs, swearing), this chapter will focus on the more positive side: modeling as being or exemplifying those abilities or the behaviors that we wish to encourage in our children. We're going to focus on the positive but, be reminded this one last time, modeling does work both ways: positive and negative behavior!

Our children are constantly watching us, looking for examples of how people—adults—are supposed to behave, look, interact with others, spend their leisure time, think and feel. When they see us living healthy and productive lives, improving ourselves, and being supportive of others, they have a tendency to act in similar ways. When they see us exhibiting laziness, greed, envy, negativity, and so on, they may likewise have a tendency to feel or act in those ways. It is far more likely that our children will model on what we do and who we really are, rather than what we tell them to do or be. Telling them to act or feel a certain way while we, their parents, do the opposite, is a weak and unreliable method of training or instruction.

THE RELEVANCE OF MODELING IN THE CONTEXT OF THIS BOOK

Modeling is an important component of encouraging potential because, as the adage goes, "actions speak louder than words." If the adults who are raising children make a habit of helping each other focus on what they can do, what they are good at, children will watch, listen, and be encouraged to behave in similar ways.

If these adults, who act as primary role models for the children they are raising, are actively and productively involved in improving themselves, then the children with whom they interact will see this and be encouraged to behave in like ways.

The sum total of most of the other, various techniques described in this book may not be as powerful as modeling.

If our children love, admire, and respect us, which is usually the case, the person that they perceive us to be is one of the most critical variables affecting who they will be.

While the topic of modeling overlaps with the topic of environmental influences discussed in Chapter 1, it is important enough to receive specific attention here. It's important because children's attitudes toward who they are and what they are capable of are significantly shaped by watching the influential adults who surround them. We've all noticed how children often grow into adults who resemble their parents in

- the way they carry their bodies and walk.
- their attitudes toward other groups of people, belief systems, political ideologies, religions, and races.
- preferred sports and leisure activities.

- favorite foods and drinks.
- attitudes toward family and child rearing.
- facial expressions and body language.

The list goes on and on. Heredity plays a very minor role in areas such as these, while the key factor is the way in which children are raised, their environment, and yes, once again, *you* are the most critical variable or factor in your children's environment. I must share here how blessed I feel that my daughter, Rachel, has somehow magically selected to model on many of the better qualities that my wife and I exemplify and, miraculously, doesn't seem to be copying very many of either of our less admirable traits—perhaps she's designing her own. Sometimes we just get lucky, I guess, but you can't really count on luck when it comes to raising children. If you have a bad habit, or habits, you have to be ready to accept the fact that your children may just decide to make them their own.

I know what you're thinking: I know lots of kids who grew up to be nothing like their parents, or even the opposite of everything their parents seemed to be. Take Johnnie Johnson. His parents were really overweight and he was as skinny as a rail. And Judy Jones. Her parents read all the time and were real intellectual and all Judy wanted to do was watch TV and play Nintendo. And Jennifer Jenkins. Her parents fought all the time, and were the meanest, nastiest people you'd ever want to meet, but Jennifer was loving, sweet, social, and as kind as could be. That's true, sometimes kids do go the opposite direction of their parents, but this isn't all that common and doesn't really alter the importance of modeling. What it does do is remind us that the best we can do as parents is our *best*. We can't know or predetermine how our efforts will turn out; we just do our best and watch and hope. Sometimes our children will decide to be or do the exact opposite from what they see us being or doing (psychologists refer to this phenomenon as *reaction formation*) but, far more often, our behavior, who and what we are, will serve as a model that they will in some way emulate. For example:

Since my daughter Rachel was born, nine years ago, she's observed me spending thousands of hours joyously playing the flute and recorder. I've taken her to dozens of concerts, exposed her to thousands of hours of classical and other types of quality music, stopped with her on street corners, parks, and fairs, to listen to dozens (or perhaps hundreds) of talented and entertaining musicians. Since she was born she has had my appreciation, love of, and dedication to music as a model. We have musical instruments all over the house and even bought a piano (neither my wife nor I play) and encouraged Rachel to play and start lessons—which didn't last long. She has had great modeling and encouragement (both encouragement and encouragement) to become involved in music. But at the present time she isn't. She does, however, have a lovely voice and does sing out loud at times, but she doesn't want to take lessons, in voice or an instrument, and doesn't seem to be progressing much in what my wife and I think may be an area of real potential, music.

Should I stop modeling my love of music? No! Should I force her to take up an instrument or voice lessons? No! Constantly and subtly encourage, but never force. Should I continue modeling for her—not to mention the real reason I'm involved in music, I love it!—and have faith that my modeling is both good for me and for her? Yes, absolutely yes!

If you love sports and physical activity and are constantly on the go, yet your children don't seem to want to use their bodies for anything other than routine activities (they aren't interested in sports or being very active), don't lose heart. You may not see the results of your modeling for five or ten or twenty or thirty years. You may not get immediate feedback that your behavior is having a positive influence on your children, but it most probably is. No guarantees, no promises, but trust me on this one— you aren't just having a good time and staying in shape, you're also being watched and evaluated. Little eyes are on you and they are gathering information about what life is about, who they are, and who and what they will someday be. The chances are good, very, very good, that you are having an impact.

We parents can control many of the ingredients that are put into our children, but we can't control what comes out (the outcomes). I have every faith in the world that even if my daughter never plays a musical instrument, never sings much in public, and never develops an interest in listening to or watching musicians play, or going to concerts, or any other type of musical events, being around me, and having my positive behavior as a model will, in some way, positively affect her.

With this self-revelation out of the way, we are now ready to look at modeling from a number of different perspectives.

- How do we, as adults, spend our time?
- How do we model the formulation and evaluation of our goals?
- How do we respond to successes and roadblocks?

HOW DO ADULTS SPEND TIME?

When you bought this book your intention was to support your children, to find ways to encourage their potential, help them be more, discover their hidden gifts, reach for the skies. You've probably figured out by now—five and a half chapters into the book—that there are a lot of things you can do to help them in these areas. You've probably also sensed by now that it's not going to be a breeze—there are a number of things you'll have to do to reach those higher outcomes you hope to attain. Well, it gets even harder now, because now I'm going to tell you that to really encourage your children, you're going to have to also work on yourself. If you want them to maximize *their* potential, you're going to need to develop *yours* too. Not a big problem for most of you probably—you bought this book and are reading it, which tells me you're a learning, growing type of person—but these next sections may be a bit challenging for those of you who were expecting an easier ride. Good luck!

How do we spend our time, and what does that mean to our children?

Parents who only occasionally watch TV and have active lives have a far better chance of raising children who will only occa-

sionally watch TV and have active lives than couch potato, five-hours-a-day TV watchers, despite what those parents tell their children to do.

Parents who have many friends with whom they share a variety of activities, get along well, and speak highly about, are encouraging their children to have friends and develop long term and positive relationships with those friends.

Parents who enjoy reading, read a lot, and encourage their children to read, have a far better chance of raising children who read more and enjoy reading than parents who merely tell their children to read and don't model the behavior.

Parents who are optimistic, have positive attitudes toward people and life, and share their thoughts and beliefs with their children, are helping to raise their children to be optimistic and positive far more than parents who don't necessarily model these attitudes but constantly tell their children, "Stop complaining," or "Just make the best of it, things don't always turn out well," or "Life stinks and you just have to learn to accept it."

Parents who eat a variety of different foods, balance their diets, eat slowly, and appreciate and savor each bite, are more assuredly teaching their children to grow into adults with similar behaviors than if those same parents were to not exhibit that behavior and instead constantly lecture, bribe, and coerce their children to act in those ways.

While not a law of nature—not an observation that can be consistently counted on—children have a tendency to develop characteristics and habits similar to those of their parents: The acorn doesn't fall very far from the tree. For example:

Children who are overweight often have at least one parent who is overweight (and, no, the reason usually is not heredity!).

Children who love and appreciate the outdoors often have at least one parent who loves and appreciates the outdoors.

Children who enjoy cooking often have at least one parent who enjoys cooking.

•••••••••••••••••••••••••••••

Children who are sensitive to poverty, discrimination, cruelty, and the plight of individuals less fortunate than they, often have at least one parent with similar views of the world.

•••••••••••••••••••••••••••••

Children who love to look at colors and designs, who have an artistic eye, often have at least one parent who sees things in this way.

There are actually a number of messages hidden in the examples given above.

1. If you wish others to be a certain way, it's a good idea to be that way yourself.

2. Actions speak louder than words.

3. Your own personal development is a critical aspect of your children's personal development.

4. Children often don't do as they're told to do (this is pretty obvious!).

What are you modeling for your children? Take a moment now and think about who you are and what you do with the seconds, minutes, hours, days, weeks, months, and years that make up your life. How do your children see you? In what ways are you a positive model for them? What attitudes or behavior do you possess that you'd rather they not model on? Think about it. You don't need to rush on to the next paragraph in a second or a minute. You can mark your place here and come back whenever you're ready. These are good questions to spend some time with. Remember: Awareness is the first step on the road to change. Becoming more aware of yourself, of who you are, how you behave, what you value, and how you live your life is a critical step in your own self-improvement, and, as this chapter is trying to impress upon you, your development is a critical, or perhaps the *most* critical, factor in encouraging your children's potential. Now, I'll write the questions for you in big, bold print, and your job is to read them, mark your place, close the book, and think:

HOW DO YOUR CHILDREN SEE YOU?

IN WHAT WAYS ARE YOU A POSITIVE MODEL FOR THEM?

WHAT ATTITUDES OR BEHAVIOR DO YOU POSSESS THAT YOU'D RATHER THEY NOT MODEL ON?

Take good care of yourself. Don't be selfish or self-centered, but watch out for yourself. How good a parent are you going to be if you can't even take care of yourself? If you don't keep your life in balance, how much and for how long are you going to be able to give to your children?

When you think or say things like this:

• •

"I've got to get into shape."

"Someday I'm going to take up golf."

"I really want to learn about the Internet and get into e-mail."

"I never have time to read. I need to make time for myself to get into some of these books I have stacked up on my desk."

"I want to go back to college someday."

"We really need to visit back home and see Grandma, Grandpa, and all the aunts, uncles, and cousins. We really need to do that soon—it's been too long!"

• •

Do you follow up? Do you just talk or do you act? Our behavior speaks much louder than our words. We may think that we are serving as good role models because we have good ideas on how we would like to be or live our lives, but it is what we actually do that teaches our children. Take marriage and our attitudes towards marriage as an example.

You often hear of or see spouses who have horrendous relationships with one another, but "stay together for the kids." While the kids may, in some ways, benefit from the family staying together, critical life lessons that are being modeled for them are that (1) sometimes in life you get stuck, and can't get out, (2) marriage is hardship, (3) we don't have the power to help ourselves, and (4) being married to someone means not getting your needs met, accompanied by coldness and/or by fighting. How we experience our marriage and relationships are models for our children.

I'm not recommending that you divorce your spouse or dump your partner. I am recommending that you take care of yourself. Remember that your children are watching you and learning from you. The way you live your life is the clearest and closest and most complete model they have of what adulthood is. Be the best, most complete person you can be, for yourself and for them.

HOW DO WE MODEL THE FORMULATION AND EVALUATION OF OUR GOALS?

While we may not at this moment actually be or have what we hope to someday be or have (our own boss, living in a big, beautiful house, at one with God, wealthy, the best tennis player in town, finished with graduate school, a great violinist), if we wish to achieve our goals it's a good idea to have both short- and long-term objectives in mind and work to accomplish them. This not only helps us become what we want to be, but also models for our children that we, as human beings, have influence over our futures, and that planning and following through with systematic schedules aimed at our own self-improvement can lead to positive results.

Many of us wish to be more in tune with God and kinder, more spiritual people. We may be far from our goals and lament that we are not better models for our children, but, at the same time, we can share with them our dreams, plans, goals, and objectives, and let them see us follow through and work our way closer and closer to where and who we wish to be. We can discuss with our children why we go to church, synagogue, or temple, and what feelings we experience and hope to experience. We can verbalize our prayers and let them witness and take part in our devotional activities and rituals.

Many of us wish to have more wealth and possessions. We may inwardly grieve (or perhaps even outwardly) that we don't have more and can't provide our children with more, but, at the same time, we can work hard, take on extra jobs, and establish savings and investment accounts. While we may never attain the specific goals we have, we can have more and share with our children our strategies for earning money, saving, and investing.

We may want to be better tennis players, but not be all that good. We can give up tennis, complain about our game or about how we started out too late in life to be really good, or we can work on improving ourselves. We can take lessons, practice, play in tournaments, and be satisfied with whatever improvement comes along. It's up to us.

One of my favorite phrases, mentioned earlier in this book, and one that I'm borrowing from a mother I overheard talking to her young son, is "Your 'I will' is going to get you a lot farther than your IQ, so get to work." Most of us have far greater potential than we'll ever realize, in many areas. It's up to us to decide which of those areas we want to devote ourselves to and then get to work.

For years my wife Marilyn and I celebrated our wedding anniversary by going to a quiet place and evaluating our previous year's contracts. We had written one-year and five-year goals for both ourselves individually, and for our relationship/ marriage. We'd discuss our previous year, the ups and downs, gains and losses, successful and less successful strategies. We'd evaluate how far we had come and make decisions on our new plans for the future. For some reason unknown to me, we have not done this recently, but I just decided I want to return to this ritual. I not only want to return to doing this with my wife, but I think it would be a great idea to share some of our plans (not all, but some) with our daughter. I think it would be excellent modeling if Rachel knew that Mom and Dad have at least one date night a week because, besides loving her, we love each other and need some time together to be close and share. I think we should let her know that we started a new savings account just for travel and the more money we have in that account by June 1, the nicer our summer vacation trip will be. And I think it would set a good example if she knew that her daddy wants to play flute in the local symphony orchestra someday but he thinks it will take him five years to get good enough and that's one reason why he's going to start taking flute lessons again and practice more.

If we want our children to plan ahead, one of the most important things for us to do is plan ahead ourselves and share those plans with them.

If your children want new baseball gloves, Nintendo games, art sets, dolls, or toys, sit down with them and set up savings programs—similar to the ones you yourselves have for retirement or summer vacations or to buy a boat or to pay for college expenses. When they reach their goals, remind them how well they did planning and saving, and help them get in touch with how good it feels to reach goals and accomplish things.

Model for your children how to break big, long-term goals into smaller, sequential objectives (such as, I want to be a great gymnast, so first I'll learn a forward and backward roll, and then a cartwheel, and hopefully by this summer, learn to do a hand-stand; I want to get a law degree, so first I'll finish my GED, then I'll enroll in the community college, eventually go to the university, and, before I die, I'll start taking night classes to be a lawyer, and finish my degree), and, when necessary, to chart or graph or in some way keep track of progress.

Delaying Gratification

One of the biggest differences between people who feel successful in life, people who accomplish things and feel a sense of pride in what they've done, and people who don't, is the ability to delay gratification—the patience to work on goals that take time to accomplish. Children need to learn that you can't always have or get what you want right away: for instance, saving money for a toy or motorcycle takes time; 15 minutes of practice, every day for one week, and you can learn to play the song beautifully; losing a pound a week for 50 weeks equals 50 pounds; the steps to becoming a brain surgeon start with tonight's homework, finishing first grade, graduating high school, and so on. They need to develop the understanding that accomplishing some goals takes a long time, and that it's helpful to break long-term goals into smaller pieces so they can track development and appreciate the smaller accomplishments along the way. The best way to learn this lesson is to see it in action, to see Mom and Dad doing it, enjoying the little victories, experiencing a sense of fulfillment and accomplishment at each little step along the way. Unless you have a specific reason not to (such as advice from your lawyer or accountant), why not share with your children the progress that's being made on retirement accounts, college funds, savings plans, the graduate degree you're working on, plans for the summer family reunion, plans for Grandma and Grandpa's 40th anniversary. If you don't share this foresight and planning with them, who will? Who can impress upon them, at a young age, that certain goals require advanced planning, saving, sacrifice, and dedication?

HOW DO WE RESPOND TO SUCCESSES AND ROADBLOCKS?

We don't always succeed, do we? We try, we labor, we push, we struggle, but sometimes it doesn't quite work out as we hope or plan that it will. When we meet with success, we celebrate, enjoy, rejoice in our accomplishments. But how do we face roadblocks? When things aren't going our way, when we feel almost out of gas, and ready to give up, how do we keep going? These are critical topics—responding to successes and roadblocks—topics that will be discussed in this section. Think about it for a moment.

■ Do most accomplishments and successes come easily?
No.

■ Must most people work hard and persist, despite
repeated failures and disappointments, in order to
reach goals of significance and worth?
Yes.

■ Do most children learn about appropriate responses to
success and failure by modeling on significant adults
in their lives?
Yes.

■ Are parents the most significant adults in most children's
lives?
Yes.

If your answers coincide with mine, you are already
understanding the significance of this topic. Let's look at some
examples of how our responses to successes and roadblocks
send messages to our children.

- *Success.* Should the single mother, who supports her two
children while working her way through school to earn her
college degree, tell her children that she was able to graduate because she worked hard, or because she was lucky?
What would each of these responses teach her children
about life?

- *Roadblock.* Should the dad who doesn't get the promotion
he wanted tell his children that he didn't get it because he's
unlucky and his boss is an obnoxious tyrant, or tell them
that now he'll just have to work that much harder so he
can earn it when the opportunity arises again? What would
each of these responses teach his children about life?

- *Success.* Should the dad who wins the two-on-two basketball championship at the city park tell his kids that he really didn't play that well and only won because the competi-
tion was lousy, or tell them how good it feels to have tried
his hardest and won? What would each of these responses
teach his children about life?

- *Roadblock.* Should the mom who has just lost an election for a seat on the school board tell her children that the city is controlled by a small clique that doesn't want her in and will never let her in, or tell them that she's still going to work hard to improve the schools and she's going to run again in the next election and win? What would each of these responses teach her children about life?

Now for the surprise answer. The answer is, whenever possible, be honest with your children, and work and hope and pray that your honest responses model a positive attitude and encourage your children to be their best. Once again, we need to be the best we can be, not only for ourselves because it feels good, but also for our children, because they watch us and think that we are how they're supposed to be.

The dilemma should now be clear: "What if I am feeling that I only graduated because I was lucky?" or "What if I feel that I didn't get the promotion because my boss is obnoxious?" "What if I played one of my worst basketball games and don't feel that good about winning?" or "What if there is a powerful clique in my town and I believe they blocked me from getting elected, and will stop me next time too?" The answer is that you must be who you are and feel what you feel but remember, your children are watching. Once again—work on yourself!

RECOMMENDATIONS

1. Be the best, most complete person you can be; your children look to you as a model of what an adult is.

2. If there are parts of yourself that you don't like and want to change, make goals for yourself, with specific short- and long-term objectives, and get to work. Help your children to see and understand that you and they have the power to change, that a person may not be perfect, but at least he or she can improve.

3. Meet together as a family, and share feelings about what's going right in your lives and things you want to change or work on. Make plans together and share joys as well as frustrations.

4. Share your strengths and achievements with your children; let them know about the good, positive, and productive things you do, but, do this in a non-pushy, non-egocentric, factual, sensitive way.

5. Be a model of perseverance; don't give up at the first feelings of frustration. Let your children see that you don't always win, or finish, or get it on the first or second try, and that most things or accomplishments worth achieving take persistence and substantial effort.

6. Don't be afraid to show your feelings. Let your children know when you're happy, frustrated, determined, angry. Let them know how you feel. Be assured that they'll watch how you deal with those feelings and your responses (modeling) will influence how they deal with their own feelings.

SUMMARY

This chapter is a combination of good news and good news. The first good news is that if we are presently exemplifying many positive personal and professional traits, our children are more than likely learning those traits from us. The other good news is that in those areas where we may not be the best of models for our children to learn from, we have the opportunity to change ourselves. We can still be models of taking responsibility for our lives, of selecting areas of ourselves we want to change, making plans, and carrying them through.

As parents we need to remember that our actions speak much louder than our words. What works best, what teaches real-life lessons to our children, is our being what we wish them to be: caring, competent, responsible, hard-working people who try to accomplish the most with what we've got, to actualize our potential in as many areas as possible.

CHAPTER 7

BUILDING RESPONSIBILITY

INTRODUCTION

W e all want our children to take responsibility for their own actions and be considerate of the needs and conditions of others, weigh those factors with their own needs, and come up with rational, reasonable, responsible decisions. It is the hope of most parents that the decisions their children make will lead them into becoming more whole and complete people, physically, psychologically, socially, spiritually, academically, vocationally and avocationally, with no (or minimal) negative effects on others.

> ## THE RELEVANCE OF BUILDING RESPONSIBILITY IN THE CONTEXT OF THIS BOOK
>
> *Critical components in enabling potential are teaching children to take chances, make sound decisions, and take responsibility for those decisions. As parents, we need to nurture and protect our children, but we also need to teach them to nurture and protect themselves. If we do too much for them, for too long, we run the risk of building an overdependence on us and creating in them the attitude—an attitude that may last, to some degree, forever—that "Mommy or Daddy will take care of me; they'll make things right." This attitude is one that encourages dependence and weakness, not potential and a strong sense of responsibility.*

LOCUS OF CONTROL, ENABLING, AND VALUES

B efore a detailed discussion of the topic of building responsibility can begin, there are some related terms that should be explained.

- *Locus of control.* We will use this term here to refer to children's perceptions of how their actions affect outcomes. Are they in control or is their life and the things that happen to them ruled by outside forces, such as parents, teachers, other children, God, luck? Some children, as well as adults, feel that what they believe and do determines the direction their lives take, that they are in charge *(internal locus of control)*. Others are convinced that their actions don't have much to do with what happens to them, that, in some way, forces outside themselves cause good and bad circumstances to arise, and they alone have very little power to correct or change that *(external locus of control)*. And, of course, most children are somewhere in between, sometimes taking credit, or responsibility for their actions, sometimes blaming others, or "bad luck," or anyone or anything outside of themselves *(mixed locus of control)*.

- *Enabling.* This is a popular term these days that refers to people or forces outside of an individual that set up an environment that makes it easier for that individual to be a certain way, or continue certain behavior. Parents who call in false excuses for their children's school absences are enabling truancy; spouses who go out every night and buy more beer for their drunken partners are enabling their alcoholism; older siblings who do everything for their younger brothers and sisters are enabling dependence and lack of self-help skills. In a positive way, parents who provide a musical instrument and music lessons for their interested children are enabling musical potential to develop; parents who provide their young children with opportunities to make decisions are encouraging decision-making abilities to blossom.

- *Values.* This term refers to those qualities, things, thoughts, and beliefs that a person or culture hold in regard, or deem to be important. Some cultures and individuals value verbal intelligence more highly than the ability to hunt game, while the opposite is true in others; some value assertiveness and personal power and magnetism, while others find these traits intrusive; some value the right to own and carry weapons, while this ancient tradition seems barbaric and out-of-date to others; some value females who are strong, confident, competent, and achieving, while others find these qualities unbecoming and perhaps even offensive.

Now, let's see if we can put these three terms together into a meaningful sentence that will sound like English as well as help to explain what in the world they have to do with building responsibility and encouraging potential. Here goes:

Parents who honestly desire to encourage potential in their children must truly value *and work on building responsibility, for it is in an* enabling *environment such as this that* internal loci *(the plural form of* locus*) of* control *are formed, which provide children with the power and confidence to propel themselves to excellence.*

I enjoyed putting that sentence together so much that I'm going to use the three terms—*locus of control, enabling,* and *values*—in another sentence, this time relating to my daughter Rachel. I'll use an example that's been on my mind lately, homework/studying:

My wife Marilyn and I value *academic achievement, learning, studying, completing assignments correctly and on time, homework, and achieving good grades, and believe that in order for our daughter Rachel to develop an* internal locus of control*/to take responsibility for her own efforts and achievements in these areas, we need to* enable *her by providing (1) enough time in her daily schedule to study and complete assignments, (2) an orderly and well-organized space in which to work, (3) role models who also* value *these things and have gained and are gaining meaning and worth through the pursuit of these* values*, and (4) reinforcement and encouragement for her efforts and the outcomes of those efforts.*

There, I think we've done it. But, just in case this concept and these terms aren't 100 percent clear, let's continue on this same topic for just a minute longer.

Before looking at some techniques for building responsibility, let's look at two children, and see how the terms and theories described above actually work in their lives.

Child #1. The parents of this eight-year-old girl have great expectations for her future, and want her to be a take-charge, I-can-do, creative, and confident adult who has a rewarding and balanced career and family life (their values). *For years they have treated their daughter as an equal partner in the family, asking for and respecting her opinions on family matters (vacations, restaurants, decorating ideas, activities), and allowed her to select her own clothing, help organize and prepare meals, plan her birthday parties and invitations, in other words,* enabling *decision making and responsibility. For years the parents and daughter have participated in regularly scheduled family meetings to make plans and to discuss the outcomes of all their major decisions, both good and bad, and point out that those outcomes were the results of decisions they themselves had made, thereby fostering an* internal locus of control.

• •

Child #2. The parents of another eight-year-old girl have minimal expectations for her future, and basically want her to stay out of trouble, remain in school until she's at least 16, and not get pregnant until she's married to someone who can support her (their values). *For years they have treated their daughter as someone who needed all decisions made for her ("You'll eat what's on the table," "Wear the clothes I tell you to," "We're going to see the new* Star Wars *movie whether you like it or not," "When you grow up you can make decisions, but not while you live in our house!"),* enabling *a passive, powerless, others-control-my-life, I'm-too-young-to-make-any-decisions attitude. For years these parents have been at odds with their daughter, constantly scolding and punishing her for not doing what she's told, rewarding her when she follows the rules, and impressing upon her a view of life that places less value or emphasis on individual efforts, and more on outside forces and doing what you're told: "That's just how life works"; "The rich get richer and the poor get _____"; "You'll have 100 years of bad luck if you sass me"; "Our family just wasn't meant to be rich or successful"; and "You do what you're told, or suffer the consequences," thereby fostering an* external locus of control.

Comparison

Now, let's compare how these two young ladies may turn out. Keep the word "may" in mind here. As has been stated often in the previous pages, how children turn out isn't a simple formula of Heredity + Environment = Child. Some children are more resilient, more able to succeed despite the hurdles and roadblocks life places before them, than others. Children respond differently to different environments.

1. Which girl was exposed to a set of *values* that is more consistent with encouraging potential? Which one will probably accomplish more in life and feel better about her accomplishments? (Answer: #1)

2. Which girl is being *enabled* to form personal attributes that will assist in encouraging potential? (Answer: #1)

3. Which girl is more likely to develop a strong *internal locus of control,* and be more courageous, creative, and confident in decision making, and taking responsibility for those decisions? (Answer: #1)

In summary, parents who truly want their children to be the most they can be—to maximize their potential—need to pay special attention to how their children are developing their sense of responsibility. These parents need to become *responsibility enablers.*

TECHNIQUES TO BUILD RESPONSIBILITY

The remainder of this chapter will focus on a number of techniques to assist parents in building responsibility in their children. These techniques include

■ providing choices.
■ building on successes.
■ letting consequences do their job.
■ including children as participants in family decisions.
■ analyzing decisions and the results of those decisions.

Provide Choices

Important points bear repeating, and, while this topic has been approached elsewhere in the book, it needs to be mentioned once again in relation to building responsibility. A critical component of building responsibility is learning to make responsible choices. From a very early age children have to make many choices.

• •

"Will I drink the milk or spill it on the floor?"

"He has my toy. Shall I grab it away from him, bite him, sit here and cry, or play with something else?"

"I see my jacket lying there on the grass, and I know I should pick it up and take it inside with me but I don't want to walk over there and I don't want to carry it. Should I get it or just let Mom or Dad do it?"

"I don't want to play with Johnnie, so should I ignore him or still say hello and smile?"

"No one's going to really know whether or not I brushed my teeth, so should I bother or just skip it?"

• •

Making responsible choices isn't a gift that children are somehow magically born with; it's learned through practice, through trial-and-error, and through living with the consequences that follow choices.

In order to learn this skill, to become responsible, children need to have lots of practice making decisions, and then living with the results of those decisions. They need to *experience.*

Some parents—not us, of course—regard their young children as not ready to make decisions. They attempt to lead, or guide, or dominate them too much, thinking that when their children get older they'll be ready to decide for themselves. These parents regard their children as too young, too unreliable, perhaps too immature to make good choices. They perhaps believe that children learn to make choices through years of being ordered about, directed, and made to behave and do as they are told. Beware of this approach.

As early as possible begin providing your children with choices, and respect their decisions. (Well, let's say respect their decisions within reason or within your own personal sense of reality.) Here are some examples.

Parent to four-month-old: "Do you want me to sing you a song?"

- *Child smiles and coos; parent says, "That sounds like a yes to me," and sings.*
- *Child makes a sad face or cries or looks away; parent says, "Okay, it looks like you'd rather not hear a song now, maybe later," and doesn't sing.*

Parent to two-year-old: "For breakfast would you rather have eggs and toast or a waffle?"

- *Child selects from choices and parent prepares it.*
- *Child comes up with another choice and parent evaluates the proposal and either agrees or discusses other options ("Yes, Honey, I understand that you'd really like to have the chocolate syrup, with some marshmallows on the side, for breakfast, but so much sugar in the morning isn't good for you. If eggs and toast or waffles don't sound good let's agree on another choice).*

Parent to four-year-old: "We're going to the mall now. You'd better bring your money if you want to shop for a toy."

- *If children don't bring money, they don't get to buy a toy.*
- *If they bring money, they can decide what toy to spend it on, and then live with their decision.*
- *If children bring money and parents forget theirs, parents can beg, and hope that the kindness they have modeled in the past will be returned!*

Parent to six-year-old: "It's your party; I'm willing to spend $50 on it, but I want you to help decide what we're going to buy and how we're going to set it up."

- *Make a list together and discuss choices and costs.*
- *Keep within the budget.*

Parents to eight-year-old: "Well, you want to go to summer camp and we need to make a decision very soon or they're all going to be full. Let's take out all the brochures we've collected and make lists of the positive and negative points for each camp. Then we can discuss the facts and make our choice. You're the one who is going to be going to the camp, so we think you should make the final decision, but we can all help figure out what your best choices would be. Let's get to work."

Practice. If you want to roller-skate well, then get in a lot of hours skating and observing and remembering what types of movements and techniques work and don't work. If you want to hit the baseball well, then get in lots of practice swinging the bat and observing and remembering what stances and types of swings yield what types of hits. If you want to raise children who act responsibly, then provide them with numerous opportunities to select from choices, and help and encourage them to evaluate and learn from choices they've made.

Build on Successes

As your children learn to make more and more responsible choices, build on their successes. When they are consistently able to select from two outfits to wear, then move to a selection from three outfits. As they learn to help you tidy up their room, provide less and less assistance and significant levels of encouragement and praise. Once they learn to care for their basic water colors set, reward them with a larger set, with more colors and a wider assortment of brushes. After they have proven that they can safely ride their bike around your small residential area, stopping at corners, looking both ways, using good judgment, consider expanding their riding area by a block or two; let them go a bit further.

In the business world, successful employers usually reward competent employees with more responsibility, pay, and benefits. So too should parents reward their children with more responsibility, choices, and allowance when they demonstrate more responsible behavior and increased ability to make wise choices.

Our goal here is to maintain at least the same level of performance, but with more and more difficult tasks (more demanding situations and choices).

For most people, repeated success teaches them that they can succeed, while repeated failure teaches them that they are failures and can't succeed. As our children meet with success in systematically arranged situations that require them to be progressively more and more responsible, they will use more and more of their potential.

Let Consequences do their Job

Chapter 3 discussed the importance of consequences in the process of encouraging potential. This is the perfect opportunity to review what we know about using consequences and to once again highlight the critical role consequences play in building responsibility.

It is the consequences of behavior that teach children (as well as adults) many important lessons in life. For example:

Dropping a toy truck from a second story window and helplessly watching as it falls to the ground and breaks into a thousand pieces (consequence) *teaches the lesson of being careful with one's possessions.*

The burning sensation (consequence) *experienced when we expose our skin to the sun for too long a period teaches us to be more cautious when outdoors.*

The low grade (consequence) *that is received on a spelling test after one week of worrying about the test but never studying the words serves as a reminder that studying pays better dividends than thinking about, considering, hoping to, or feeling guilty about not studying.*

The father's expression of pain and displeasure (consequence) *and the subsequent task of apologizing and cleaning the dirt off Daddy's pants and the floor* (consequence) *teach a child not to throw a dirt-filled planter as a joke.*

The stomachache (consequence) *that might follow eating an entire chocolate cake reminds us to be more responsible in our consumption of sweets.*

We don't want our children injured or emotionally damaged, and therefore we make every effort to teach them, model for them, and surround them with safe environments. However, after our children have erred, we need to allow consequences to do their jobs—teach responsibility and accountability. We need to allow natural consequences, those that emerge from experimentations and interactions in life (such as not paying attention and walking into a wall, leaving a bike in the driveway and having it stolen, smearing ink on a favorite shirt and having a permanent stain on the shirt) do their job. We also need to devise and employ logical consequences with our children for situations in which they demonstrate inappropriate behavior and lack of responsibility (cutting up a doll with a scissors, poor grades or report card, not completing household jobs, breaking a promise). Parents, especially very nurturing and protective ones, need to beware of the tendency to "make it all better," soothe the pain, take care of it. We need to let our children experience life's lessons. If we work too hard at protecting them from consequences, we are enabling behaviors that we really should not be promoting, and are helping them develop an external locus of control.

The message is clear: Use consequences.

- Don't let your children get run over by cars but if they leave a toy in the driveway and a car runs over it, have them clean up the mess and replace the toy with their own money.

- Encourage your children to remember to bring their "show and tell" to school but if they forget it, don't take time out of your day to bring it to them. Okay, I did break this rule once—my daughter forgot to take her Barbie doll on the bus for show and tell, so I dropped it off on my way to work. She called home and was crying and upset—I was weak and spineless. I did it, saved her. But, I must admit that my intervention was but a short-term solution to a long-term lesson in life. The lesson: Don't leave home without your Barbie!

- When they are handling their ice cream cone carelessly, and the ice cream falls off and drops to the sidewalk, be sympathetic, but don't go buy them another one, or give them yours. (Well, this may be another

example of me not always following my own advice;
but, in my own defense, you need to know that those
times I did buy my daughter second ice cream cones,
I did it with full knowledge and understanding that I
was enabling her carelessness and not providing ideal
support to the development of her internal locus of
control.)

Do you want to have to check the driveway for toys five
times a day? Act as your child's personal valet? Have them dropping food and drinks on floors and sidewalks all over the country? (If you're thinking this is a pretty good description of your
life as it exists, then I recommend that after finishing this book,
you take a close look at the bibliography in the back and consider reading one or more of the books that focus on building
responsibility.) If so, don't let consequences do their job; solve
their self-made problems for them. If not, be warm and compas-
sionate when they suffer the consequences of poor decisions
and irresponsible acts, but don't go too far, too often, to make
things right.

Include Children as Participants in Family Decisions

As children grow and develop, their worlds expand from
inside the confines of their own bodies to home and family and
beyond. It is within the home, with their own family, that most
children learn how life works—how people get along with one
another—and begin to understand what it means to be a person
and a social being.

Parents who include their children, from early on in life,
as fellow democratic decision makers, are giving them a huge
head start in the development of their sense of responsibility.

Many believe, myself included, that one of the major reasons adolescents tend to rebel against their parents is because
they desire more of what has been denied them for 12 or 13 or
14 years, namely, more self-determination and responsibility,
more respect for who they are and what they believe, and more

occasions when they are consulted regarding decisions that affect them. Perhaps if we parents allowed our children more of a voice in selecting their clothes and hairstyles, as adolescents they would be less likely to choose clothes and hairstyles we regard as wild and crazy; or picking types and destinations of family vacations, as adolescents they would be more likely to want to go on vacations with us; or delineating and dividing up household chores, as adolescents they would be more likely to participate in cooking, cleaning, and straightening up without being pushed, prodded, and threatened.

I can't quote much research to support the possible outcomes just described but they make sense, don't they?

Many parents who do provide their children with more freedom to direct their own lives, determine their likes and dislikes, and assume responsibility, report that at first the process is very threatening, but after they've gained more experience with it, their home lives have become much easier, primarily due to their creation of less dependent and more confident children who are more willing to assume responsibility and help out. If this approach attracts you, I strongly recommend you purchase a copy of Rudolf Dreikurs' book entitled *Family Council* (see the Bibliography, page 240), and learn more about incorporating children in family decisions.

Analyze Decisions and the Results of those Decisions

Whether children are given just a bit more power over their own lives or are actually included as equal partners in the family structure, a critical element of their learning from the experience of having more responsibility is our modeling for them and in other ways assisting them in analyzing the results of their decisions. To learn from experiences we need to look at the various outcomes of those decisions. We need to evaluate the varying effects (on our present condition, on our future, and on others around us) or results of what we have done.

Parents can do this by modeling self-evaluation for their children. For example:

Dad hurriedly plants a new bed of flowers in the yard and all the flowers die two weeks later. Looking at the flowers with the children present, Dad says, "Well, I guess this is what happens when you try to do something the easy way. I should have put some richer dirt in with this old dry clay (holds up a handful of poor soil), and I should have sprayed some insect killer around (points to swarms of bugs eating the leaves). Next time I'm going to do a better job!"

• •

Mom and children are driving away from the car lot in their brand-new, four-wheel drive, king cab truck. Mom says, with a big smile on her face, "The moral of this story is save for things you really want. Those pennies, nickels, dimes, and quarters can add up. You know our piggy bank on top of the refrigerator? It's been eight years that we've been saving all our change, putting it in that little piggy, and moving the money from there to our special savings accountant at the bank—our truck account. Saving that change didn't take anything away from what we had, or how we lived our life, and look what it got us, eight years later. Incredible!"

• •

Parent lets out a shriek of joy that rings throughout the house: "I made it; I did it; I'm there!" Pointing to a chart hung above the bathroom scale, the parent, beaming from ear to ear, reviews with the children the information on the chart. Fifty-two marks on the graph reveal that the parent has lost an average of one pound per week over the past year. The line descends into a picture of a thin and muscular young person, and a caption that reads Time for a New Wardrobe.

Action (modeling) speaks much more strongly than lecturing but, strongest of all, is modeling behavior, and, when appropriate, honestly and openly discussing your motivations and analyzing, in front of your children, the outcome of your behavior.

How can we help our children to analyze the results of their decisions without being too pushy or making it sound like a lecture? The key ingredients here are (1) be subtle, (2) take time, and (3) listen.

Being *subtle* means trying to get your children to come up with an evaluation without asking direct questions. Examples might include the following.

- *Not subtle.* "So, you jumped in the puddle and got your shoes all wet and now you're cold. That wasn't a smart thing to do, was it?! You aren't going to do it again, are you?"

- *Subtle.* "You look cold, Honey." And, perhaps add, "I'll bet you wish you hadn't jumped in that puddle."

- *Not subtle.* "Let me get this straight. He took your ball away, so you called him a dumb idiot, grabbed the ball back, and shoved him, and that's when he hit you and cut your lip. That was a pretty stupid way of getting your ball back! What's a better way?"

- *Subtle.* "That sure was the rough way of getting your ball back." (followed by silence, during which time the child will hopefully think, and perhaps respond).

- *Not subtle.* "Didn't I tell you that if you didn't study for your spelling test you would miss a lot of words? Now look at this grade!"

- *Subtle.* "You look so sad! Oh, I see, it's your spelling test. You don't look very happy about it!"

One of the most difficult ways to get children to think and talk is by asking questions. A subtle, nonaccusing comment or observation, followed by silence, often helps them reflect more, and participate in discussion with you more willingly.

This approach takes time, but the chances of getting your children to think and analyze are greatly improved. Just by sitting there quietly, attentively, and patiently, waiting for them to initiate the conversation, you may well encourage more sharing than from all the questions in the world.

When they do start talking, listen. Listen to their words and the feelings behind their words. Listen without judgment or criticism. Listen as if you were a tape recorder or a mirror, rather than a judge or psychiatrist. The closer you listen, the more they'll talk and, the more they talk, the better the chances that they will become more effective and efficient evaluators of their own behavior, the better the chances that their encounter with you—you, the listener—will help them grow.

RECOMMENDATIONS

1. Remember that children who consistently behave more responsibly often have a strong internal locus of control; they hold themselves responsible for all or most of the outcomes of their actions.

2. Help your children build a strong internal locus of control by modeling it yourself, and also by encouraging them to evaluate how their actions caused results or outcomes to occur.

3. Enable your children to tap into their potential, rather than to be dependent on you. Beware of making a habit of helping them out of situations their own behavior has caused. When you do step in, be aware that in solving the short-term problem you may not be helping in the long-term solution.

4. Your own values are an important determinant of how your children will learn to perceive themselves, their goals, and the world around them. Be aware of your values and what you are subtly teaching your children.

5. Allow, encourage, and set up situations in which your children can make choices. Making wise choices is a skill that needs practice, and the earlier one begins the better.

6. Set up situations that build on your children's successes. When they've mastered a certain skill move on to the next skill, or make the task a little more difficult, not so difficult that they won't succeed, but enough to challenge them.

7. Use consequences and, without adopting an "I told you so" attitude, make an effort to make sure your children see the cause-and-effect relationship between their actions and subsequent consequences.

8. Include your children as participants in family discussions and decisions.

9. Let your children see how you analyze the outcomes of your actions and decisions, and encourage them to do the same.

SUMMARY

To help your children come as close as possible to using all the potential they have inside them, it is of critical importance to focus on their abilities to make sound and responsible choices, to live with the consequences of those choices, and to evaluate the outcomes. We can and should model this behavior, as well as set up environments where our children can accomplish these things and experience success.

CHAPTER 8

CARE PROVIDERS
AND TEACHERS

INTRODUCTION

Most children spend a great deal of time under the supervision and educational guidance of adults other than their parents. Teachers (for purposes of this chapter this group includes day care providers, as well as pre- and elementary school teachers) can have significant influences on children. Keeping this in mind, it's a good idea for parents to know what qualities to look for in these individuals, so they can see to it that their children are spending their time in the best possible environment.

THE RELEVANCE OF CARE PROVIDERS AND TEACHERS IN THE CONTEXT OF ENCOURAGING POTENTIAL

As was discussed in the chapters on potential and encouragement (Chapters 1 and 2), children enter this world with different amounts of potential in different areas, and different degrees or types of sensitivities to the environments they encounter (differing levels of need for encouragement). Some children have such incredible potential, and need so little outside encouragement that they will flourish despite a poor teacher, while others balance near the edge, a hair breadth away from becoming motivated and turned on to be their best, and that same hair breadth away from giving up and settling for an easier path, a path in which they will only take advantage of a small portion of their potential.

Because it is usually impossible for parents to be sure which group their children fall into, they must do all they can to assure that their children spend as much time as possible with teachers and other role models who will provide enriching and supportive environments. The following pages will clarify what parents should look for in these teachers, and provide some options for parents who find their children in less than ideal settings.

WHAT TO LOOK FOR IN A GREAT TEACHER

Teaching is neither a science nor an art, but both. Great teachers need to be aware of and able to put to use research in child and human development, motivation, reading, writing, math, science, art, music, physical education, and more. They need to understand how children learn and how to set up environments to encourage that learning. At the same time, they must be artists and entertainers, constantly thinking of creative and interesting ways to motivate children to practice skills they have not yet mastered, become interested in achieving goals they don't truly understand, and continue performing, striving, and achieving, despite the weather, time of year, and other, sometimes overwhelming distractions.

Few teachers become masters at all aspects of learning and teaching (hopefully we can each think of two or three such teachers from our past, but many adults have difficulty remembering any teachers like this). Most teachers, in fact, most human beings, have areas of greater and lesser strength, things they do well and things they do less well. Unfortunately, some teachers do few things well, and also are capable of doing a number of damaging things to children, things that negatively affect children's learning and self concepts.

This chapter will describe six positive characteristics parents should look for in their children's teachers. These six characteristics do not represent the entirety of teaching—there are many other important skills—but they do represent key elements that will help to encourage your children's potential. These elements include the following.

1. When you're around these adults, what general feeling or vibration do they emit—magnetism/charisma? Do they seem happy or sad, optimistic or pessimistic, encouraging or discouraging, animated and alive, or dull and boring?

2. Are they well organized, and how does that organization reflect their values? Do they know and have records that support which children are working at what levels and what learning will follow after mastery has been reached? What are their beliefs, their philosophy regarding working with young children?

3. Are students asked to spend much of their time working on tasks, projects, or assignments that they have either already mastered or that are far too difficult for them? Or are they usually involved in tasks, projects, and assignments that are at their level, that they haven't quite mastered, but are close enough to keep their motivation up and keep them learning?

4. Does all learning that takes place have to happen in the same way for all children (for example, all listening to the teacher and then answering oral questions to show they understand, or all reading and summarizing materials, or, all working independently at centers, or, all doing seat work— work on their own, at their seats)? Or are children allowed to approach subjects in different ways, to sometimes play or study alone and sometimes in groups, to sometimes write or draw on paper and sometimes in the sand or on chalk-boards, to sometimes answer questions in writing, sometimes orally, or perhaps sometimes through movement?

5. Are children with special interests (stamps, ballet, soldiers, railroads) allowed to bring their special interests into the center or school and learn other topics through their interests?

6. Do your children like the home, or center, or school you take them to and the activities they are involved in there? Or is it a constant struggle to get them to leave home in the morning and a continuing challenge to get them to say anything positive at the end of their day?

These are the positive characteristics that parents should be searching for in their children's teacher. These are the building blocks of excellence, each of which will be discussed in greater detail.

GENERAL FEELING

This topic needs to be handled very carefully and clearly. There are many teachers with great magnetism or charisma who are only average or perhaps even below average teachers. There are also many teachers who are excellent but don't have the flair or exciting mystique that one might call magnetism/charisma. Now that all these warnings and disclaimers have been made, the keys or questions are: (1) Is this a teacher that can attract the interest of children and motivate them to learn? and (2) Does this person really care about the children; about who they are and who they will someday become? Is this person a positive role model for children?

Magnetism/Charisma

Sometimes magnetism/charisma is a very egocentric thing, an outpouring of personality, positiveness, creativity, and humor whose sole purpose is to make a good impression, to tell others that "I'm a great person." This is not the magnetism/charisma we're looking for in our children's teachers. What we're looking for is a sense of warmth and caring, an ability to entice and motivate young learners, a vibration that says, "I really like kids and I like my job. I hope that being the positive, creative, open person that I am will connect with you, and that together we can learn and grow and still have fun and joy along the way."

A teacher who leaves others with these feelings, is honest, and has the teaching skills that will be described below, can really help to bring out potential that might otherwise lay dormant and silent. This trait can act as a catalyst to bring children to new self-awareness and new experiences.

The best judges of a teacher's magnetism/charisma are often children. They know what appeals to them and what doesn't. You may be positively affected by a certain school or class or teacher, while your children are hardly, or perhaps even negatively impressed. Listen to them; watch them. Not always, but often, their openness or caution, like or dislike, or good feelings or concerns may foreshadow something that you aren't aware of or sensitive to. Your children's reactions may just be initial attraction or trepidation, but they should not be ignored.

In the case of negative magnetism, or disturbing personality traits (such as nervousness, anger, disinterest, or a low energy level), you usually want to look for another teacher. First impressions aren't 100 percent reliable, but they are often the best information we have. While discarding a possible program or teacher after only one meeting may sometimes be a mistake, it is often a wise decision and one that still leaves the door open in your search for excellence.

ORGANIZATION

H ow organized are the teachers and how does that organization reflect their values?

● ●

Do they group students, and, if so, how?

How and why do groups change?

What kind of records do they keep?

What's their daily schedule like?

What do they do with children who master a game, activity, or skill before the other children, or perhaps before it's even introduced?

● ●

These are the types of questions parents should be asking and searching for prior to enrolling their children in a program. Ideally, the teachers will do more than talk; they will show you schedules, lists, charts, and record books, and explain how they do things.

Once again, this area isn't everything (a well-organized teacher may not be a good teacher and a teacher who is less well-organized may not be all that bad a teacher). No, organization isn't everything, just one more of the many ingredients you need to be looking for.

The ways in which teachers structure or organize their programs may also reflect their value systems. Keep in mind here that you're better off knowing what *you* value before deciding whether or not you like what *they* value. For example:

Some teachers like to give their students many repetitive, short-duration, right-answer-focused, fill-in-the-blanks, do-as-you're-told-type assignments. They evaluate or grade children on correct responses, and/or speed, and/or accuracy. Some parents like this: "They keep my kid working and on task!" I personally would prefer more open-ended assignments where my daughter is given the opportunity to think and solve more realistic life problems. The teachers here are well-organized, but our values are different.

. . . .

Some teachers organize their programs by placing children in groups by age, or according to high, middle, or low ability or performance. Each group works at a different level and children in one group rarely interrelate with those in other groups. For some parents this type of organization seems great; it's clear, easy to understand, lowers frustration on the part of some kids, and makes expectations clearer. I personally would rather my daughter was in an educational setting where she wasn't grouped so often or in such an unchanging way. I like to see kids relate more with all ages, types, and levels of peers, and at times to work outside of groups, perhaps with partners or on independent assignments. The teachers in this example are well organized, but we don't hold the same values.

. . . .

Some teachers organize their homework in such a way that parents are asked or required to work for 15, 30, or 45 minutes every night on specific assignments with their children. The teachers may be well organized but, on a day-to-day basis, I'd much prefer to work or play at home on activities of our own choosing, rather than on the assignments determined by the teacher. I'd like to read to and be read to, to write with, and to play with my daughter. I enjoy and cherish times we have that are spontaneous and fun, and prefer to incorporate practice and new learning into our own streams of creativity and self-expression. I realize that once children enter kindergarten or first grade they may have homework but I don't want to completely give up activities we enjoy doing together in order to meet teachers' demands. Once again, the teachers may be well organized, but the organization doesn't quite suit my, or our, needs.

Ask to see how the teachers keep records. What do they look for? What information do they record? How do they share this information with parents? All are important questions.

Learn what type of organizational structure your children's prospective teachers have, and what their values are—do they fit you, your children, and your family?

CHALLENGE VERSUS REPETITION VERSUS FRUSTRATION

Are children working on new and challenging tasks? Are they perhaps repeating old learning or being frustrated by activities that are too difficult? Look carefully at the toys, games, books, and activities that will surround your children in their new educational setting. Will they be interested, challenged, and motivated? Does this look like an environment that will turn your children on? You know better than anyone else what motivates them, what bores them, what frightens them, and what holds their interest. Does this look like the kind of environment that's right for them? If your answer is "sort of," "kind of," "maybe," or "I'm not sure," then keep looking. You're making an important decision that should not be rushed.

While it's often beneficial to have children of various ages and/or abilities interacting with one another, you need to evaluate if the overall atmosphere is below, at, or above your children's level. Consider the following.

Will your infants be in a day-care center surrounded by three- and four-year-olds, spending long hours confined in a crib or walker, to protect them from materials that are inappropriate for them or from other children who might hurt them? If so, not good!

Will your three-year-olds, who hold crayons and pencils in a closed fist and scribble wildly, be provided with coloring book pages and thin crayons and be asked to color neatly inside the lines? If so, not good!

Will your five-year-olds, who are already reading and writing at the mid-first grade level, be forced to sit in large groups with other kindergartners and practice reading and writing their ABCs? If so, not good!

Will your six-year-olds, who don't have any homework, be forced to sit at a desk and do schoolwork for the first hour of the afterschool care program because most of the kids have homework and the program insists that children do schoolwork for the first hour, every day? If so, not good!

Will your eight-year-olds, who are still having difficulty with addition and subtraction, be forced to move on to multiplication and division, because that's what's in the workbook and all the kids have to stay together? If so, not good!

The central issue here is appropriateness, both for your children's age levels and for their own particular strengths and needs. It's not all that hard for teachers to establish learning environments that are appropriate for a wide range of abilities and interests. Your children should not have to repeat previously mastered learning or be frustrated with new learning or activities that they are not prepared for just because they're a certain age or because it's easier for the teacher to structure things in that way. For example:

If your eighteen-month-olds don't mouth objects that they touch, never try to swallow things they shouldn't, and enjoy and benefit from playing with preschool toys that have smaller parts, then a big and bold "WAY TO GO!" for the day-care and preschool teachers who let them play in the big kids' area with those games and materials that aren't supposed to be safe for infants and toddlers. Good for them!

If your three-year-olds know the names of all the letters and want to start learning the sounds and how to read, hopefully their teachers will provide them with materials and assist them. While this would be unnecessary and inappropriate for most three-year-olds, the teachers here are looking at children as individuals, and providing them with what they want and need. Good for them!

If your six-year-olds don't know their letters or show any interest in reading, hopefully their teachers will not force them to read books. Ideally, the teachers will provide them with more fundamental activities to prepare them for the more formal reading that will come later. They will encourage skills as they emerge and will not force expectations on your child. (The Hurried Child, *by David Elkind, speaks beautifully to this issue. See Bibliography, page 240.) If you see teachers doing this,* Good for them!

If your eight-year-olds already know how to do a certain computer program, and the teachers are about to teach that program to the other students in the class, my commendations to the teachers for letting your children go off on their own and experiment with different ways to use the program and expand on their knowledge, rather than making them stay with the group and relearn the program. Good for them! *(Is it any wonder that many children who are actually gifted are labeled by teachers as behavior problems and/or having attention-deficit/hyperactivity disorders?)*

Far too many young learners with special gifts and talents never tap into their potential because they get bored in their educational environments and are not given the opportunity to push or challenge or express themselves. They are asked to do things they already know how to do, to study material that they have already mastered, to stay with the group and be a part of the team even though the group or team is moving incredibly slowly and holding them back.

Far too many young learners who are late bloomers never approach their potentials because they are pushed and prodded too soon, made to feel like failures, and develop low, "I can't do it" self concepts. They are forced into age-level, or grade-level expectations that don't fit them and their unique sequence of unfolding. Is every tree expected to bloom on the first day of spring? No. Some bloom earlier and some later. Is every tank of gasoline that's put in a car supposed to yield 15 to 25 miles per gallon? No. Cars differ; driving conditions differ; drivers differ. Then I ask you, why do so many parents and teachers expect and sometimes even demand that

• •

all twelve-month-olds stand, take their first step, and say their first word?

all three-year-olds speak in sentences, begin hopping on one foot, and count to ten?

all five-year-olds learn to recite their ABCs, write their names clearly, and learn to skip?

all seven-year-olds read at the first-grade level, understand basic addition, and have the ability to sit and attend to boring lectures for 20 to 30 minutes?

• •

We want people working with our children who will accept them for who they are and what level they're at, who will provide them with learning environments that will be sensitive to their levels of individual ability and achievement and take them from there, one step at a time, to higher levels. What you want to find in a classroom or educational environment is (1) children working with materials that are appealing to their age level (age appropriate), and (2) children working at or on tasks that interest, motivate, and challenge them to stretch their abilities (individually appropriate).

Most day-care centers, preschools, and primary grade classrooms are consciously designed to meet the needs of the children in the middle, those who are neither advanced nor those who have special learning needs or delays. If your children aren't right near the middle, if they possess areas in which they are advanced or have particular interests, or if they need extra reinforcement or a different type of learning experience—you need to be especially careful to find teachers and classrooms that will be appropriate for them. (This topic is discussed in more detail in Chapter 11.) Keep in mind that

- ■ most two-year-olds don't want to learn the names of every type of monkey on earth, but if your two-year-olds do, hopefully their teachers will encourage their curiosity and supply them with books and pictures that will assist them in their quest for knowledge.
- ■ most four-year-olds don't put small, nonedible objects in their mouths and swallow them, but if your four-year-olds do, then the typical day-care center or preschool program will need to be flexible to meet their "special need."
- ■ most five-year-olds can sit for five to ten minutes and listen to instructions or information without standing up and walking around, but if your five-year-olds have difficulty doing this, they will need to be in a kindergarten that makes special allowances for that particular need.
- ■ most six-year-olds have not been fascinated by mechanical devices for their entire lives, and don't spend hours a day analyzing how things work and seeing life and relationships as mathematical or logical formulas, but if your children do, hopefully their teachers will build on this strength, and incorporate it in new learning, rather than regard it as something that needs to be focused on only at home, or in private lessons.
- ■ most eight-year-olds don't need a full minute to formulate a one-sentence response or question and verbalize it, but if your eight-year-olds stutter or have other language difficulties, or are very nervous talking in front of others, hopefully their teachers will be patient, and give them the time to speak, without being hurried or made to feel different or guilty.

A VARIETY OF APPROACHES

How do students spend their time? Are they provided with a variety of approaches to teaching and learning? Some children (this applies to adults too) prefer working alone, while others love being in groups. Some remember better when they use their eyes; others rely more on their ears. Some are very logical, mathematical, and dominated by reason, others tend to see things philosophically or artistically and are more in tune with feelings and emotions. Kids (and adults) are all different; they see the world in different ways and learn new information more readily with one approach than another.

Starting when children are at the age of about three, many educational programs begin relying more and more on providing information and new learning through children's eyes and ears ("watch and listen"). Children are expected to sit for longer and longer periods of time and begin fitting into an educational system more and more like high school or college. They are asked to listen to and watch the teacher and then answer questions either orally or with paper and pencil. This may work fine for some children, but for many needs go unmet when this approach is taken. After spending years learning and enjoying experiences through using their senses of smell, taste, touch, movement, and balance, far too many preschoolers, kindergartners, and primary grade children are asked to save those senses for recess, or lunchtime, or perhaps after school, and focus on the information they are receiving through their eyes and ears.

It's not surprising that so many children, the moment they are released from the academic preschool or elementary school classroom, run about here and there, experiencing all the senses they were asked to keep in check while in the classroom. The younger the child, the more these other senses need to be included in learning. Wait—I take it back; forget the age of the child. Many older children and adults would be provided great benefit if new learning incorporated the use of many different sensory inputs. Look around the educational environment in which you have placed or are about to place your children. Are teachers taking advantage of possible learning opportunities other than those presented through the visual and auditory channels? If not, why not?

Besides the senses that might be brought into play in approaching new learning, also look for various styles or approaches. Many children, many learners, don't gain as much understanding from listening and/or watching as they do from solving real-life problems. Many can tell you what they think much better than they can answer true-false and multiple-choice questions. Many have too much energy in their bodies to sit for extended periods of time, and need to get up, move around, and become actively, physically involved to stimulate their other senses so they are prepared to receive information, understand, and remember. Some enjoy playing games so much that almost any type of new information, new learning, can be made more available to them if translated into a game format. Flexibility, meeting the needs of children in a way that will motivate them, variety, openness…look for these qualities, these approaches.

You as a Learner

Think of yourself for a moment. How do you learn best? Through your eyes or ears? Reading or listening? Actively involved or passively? Alone or with one other person or in groups? Through real-life simulations or games? From part to whole or from whole to part? Do you have particular strengths in how you learn? Any weaknesses?

Now that you're more aware of yourself as a learner, think about your children. Look at the questions in the previous paragraph and answer them for your children. Slow down a minute and really think about how they learn best. Put this book down for just a minute—or perhaps longer—and think about the messages your children have sent you about how they learn best and least well.

Good—after reflecting I trust that you now have a somewhat clearer picture regarding your children's learning styles and yours. Knowledge and awareness are powerful tools in helping us grow. Let's go on. Let me repeat some important points.

Most children (and adults) can and do learn in a combination of ways. They have preferred styles, or approaches, but can take in information, understand it, and remember it pretty easily regardless of the type of instruction they receive. Put these children into any reasonable learning environment and they progress.

This flexibility is not there, however, in all children. Some do not do very well when forced to use only their listening skills or when made to gather information by just watching or reading. Some children need to use their bodies and move around, while others learn best when new information enters their minds in rhyme or poetry or through music or rhythm. Seems strange, doesn't it? Well, it's true.

This applies to *all* children, to some degree, not just those who have learning disabilities, or mental retardation, or blindness, or hyperactivity. The issue is getting the most we can out of young learners, meeting their needs in the best possible ways so that they can learn and grow.

Look for teachers and classrooms that do this. Look for variety and creativity in approaches to learners. For some kids this may not be critical but it will help them. For others this is very critical, and, if forced to learn in ways they aren't good at, they may never realize one tenth of their potential, and they and you may never know that it wasn't their ability or potential that limited them, but how they were taught.

SPECIAL INTERESTS

Are your children allowed and encouraged to pursue their special interests during school? Some teachers go out of their way to discover the interests of their children and design a curriculum around those areas. These teachers are well aware that the best way to teach is to first find out what those you are teaching want to learn, to find topics that the children either know and want to learn more about, or topics that motivate and excite them but about which they know very little. Here are some examples.

Some one-year-olds aren't very interested in picture books, but love to touch different textures and push and pull on things that make different sounds. These are the children who can be initially enticed into becoming interested in words, stories, and literature through the use of multisensory books that have many things to touch and buttons to push to make different sounds.

Some three-year-olds love trucks, so why not work on the words and concepts of above/below, between/beside, in front/behind, larger/smaller, first/second/third..., over/under, *while playing with those trucks?*

All the five- and six-year-olds in the kindergarten class are excited because the circus is coming to town, so the teacher decides to bring the circus into the classroom by studying all about different aspects of the circus during the week preceding and the week following the circus performance.

A group of seven-year-olds love Barbie dolls. The teacher designs learning centers and educational activities where students can write about and to Barbie, design Barbie clothes, compute Barbie math problems, create Barbie diets (these would, of course, all need to be under 1,000 calories a day, and ensure the maintenance of her 1-inch waistline!), contemplate how Barbie's life would be different if she were a person of color, or from another country or culture. (Of course we could design the same learning centers and educational activities around Ken, or Ranger Rick, or the Incredible Hulk!)

• •

Five eight-year-olds are talking about building a clubhouse in a backyard. Could they not—perhaps during math time—draw pictures of the clubhouse and calculate how much wood and other materials it would take to build it?

As all parents are aware, getting children interested and motivated is more than half the battle of learning something new. Disinterested, unmotivated children are hard to teach, but if you begin with their natural curiosity and interests, and mix the curriculum or goals into that, learning usually flows quickly and easily.

When investigating a center or classroom for your children, look around and see what's going on, what the kids are doing. Look at their faces, feel their energy, listen to them conversing with one another. You'll soon be able to tell if the interest is there or not. You'll be able to tell if the curriculum is coming from the children's interests or that of the teachers.

LIKING SCHOOL

I f your children enjoy their center/school, talk about it a lot at home, and are excited with the projects and activities they are involved with, congratulations; all is probably going well. If they don't, if it's hard to get them going and out the door in the morning, if they don't want to talk about their daily experiences, and/or if they complain a lot, there *may* be a problem. The *may* is important here. It just *may* be that they love staying home, and being with you; or, they *may* like their center/school, but not the bus; or, they *may* like the bus and school, but...The idea here is that you should investigate before jumping to conclusions.

Learning does not have to be, and rarely is, all fun and games, but most learning takes place a lot faster and easier, especially for young children, when there is fun, excitement, and motivation. If it isn't there for your children, you need to look into what's going on and evaluate whether or not they're in the right learning environment.

IF THE CENTER/SCHOOL OR TEACHER IS LESS THAN ACCEPTABLE

- *Preventive measure before enrollment.* Before enrolling your children in a program or with a teacher, gather as much information as you can. Who are the teachers? How do they teach? How do they treat children? Whenever possible go and observe them in action. Talk to parents who have had children in that program, and to the children themselves (remember to be subtle or you'll just get the answers you want to hear).

- *Once your child is already participating in the program— approach #1.* If possible, volunteer to help in the program and try to both pick up information and help the teachers.

Attempt to assist them in specific areas that are bogging them down or holding them back.

- *Approach #2.* Use straightforward communications that express what it is that you like and don't like, and why. Express your concerns to the teachers and attempt to come up with a solution or solutions that will meet their needs, your needs, and the needs of your children.

- *Approach #3.* Encourage the teachers to make special arrangements for your children's areas of special needs (abilities or disabilities). This might include going to a class with older, more advanced, or younger, less advanced students for a certain time of the day or for certain subjects, spending more time outside, extra opportunities to work on puzzles, or play with blocks, or experiment with the computer—whatever they need!

- *Approach #4.* Make an effort to have your children's needs met through outside classes and activities. Ideally, this should be done in addition to having your children in a great program or class, rather than as a substitution for a less than adequate situation. This doesn't solve any problems in school but is often necessary.

- *Next to last resort.* Speak to the director or principal about your concerns.

- *Last resort.* Move your children to a different program, or ask that your children's class assignment be changed.

RECOMMENDATIONS

1. Prior to registering, go to the day-care center or preschool or primary classroom with your children and meet the teachers. Ideally, both you and your children will feel good about the program and the people; they'll impress you in a positive way.

2. If you or your children have any uneasy feelings about the program or people, take heed. First impressions are often very revealing, and many children are extremely good at sensing which adults they will work well with and which they won't.

3. Look for teachers who seem organized and can clearly explain what they're doing and why. Ideally, they will be good record keepers who know how their students are performing and can support this with data.

4. Learn what the teachers' values and goals are. Ideally, your values and goals will be similar.

5. Check to be sure that the materials and curriculum are at your children's level—not too easy and not overly demanding is ideal.

6. Determine whether the teachers teach and allow children to learn in a variety of different ways, or if it is one program for all, despite what an individual may need. Decide if your children, with their unique learning preferences, will fit in here.

7. Investigate and learn if the program is based on the teachers' interests and the materials they have available, or on what your children are really motivated by.

8. Find out if the program is flexible enough to incorporate the particular needs and preferences of your children.

SUMMARY

A mong the most critical decisions you will make regarding your children's future are if and where they will participate in day-care or preschool programs, and who will be their teachers in the primary school grades.

Parents have the choice of being passive recipients of whatever comes their way—the neighbor as day-care provider, followed by the nearest and cheapest preschool, and then whatever teachers the elementary school principal selects. Or they can take an active role in choosing where and who will serve as models and teachers of their children. The first approach is *not recommended.*

Take charge parents! Talk to other parents, interview children, go and observe and speak to day-care providers, preschool directors, principals, and teachers. Demand the best that's out there for your children, and if you don't like what you find, don't accept it. Work to change it. Your children are depending on you, and remember: *Your decisions in the first few years of your children's lives are the most important educational decisions you will ever make.*

CHAPTER 9

TEACHING/TUTORING TECHNIQUES TO WORK EFFECTIVELY WITH YOUR CHILD

INTRODUCTION

C hapter 4 discussed techniques for following the lead of your children and positively redirecting their attention. It is now time to introduce a number of other basic teaching/ tutoring techniques parents can use to encourage learning. This chapter is not meant to be a comprehensive teaching/tutoring guide; rather, it is a listing and discussion of a number of theories, approaches, and techniques that can be used either together, as an overall approach, or separately, as assorted recipes in a cookbook, to help make experiences with your children more enjoyable for both of you, and educationally enriching for them.

THE RELEVANCE OF TEACHING AND TUTORING TECHNIQUES IN THE CONTEXT OF THIS BOOK

Your teaching and tutoring techniques are not the most critical variables in encouraging the potential of your children. You can actually be a rather mediocre or poor teacher/tutor yourself and still do a great job of encouraging potential. The good news is that identifying areas of potential, encouraging, using consequences rather than punishment, following their lead, supporting the emerging skills philosophy, modeling, fostering a strong sense of responsibility, and selecting your children's teachers, in the vast majority of cases are all more important than your own ability to serve as the teacher, or tutor, or guide.

Your job is to provide as rich, stable, and positively challenging an environment as possible, but you don't need to be the one to coax or push all the knowledge and skills into their little heads.

Then, "Why include this section in the book?" you may ask. The reason is because there will be many opportunities for you to teach and tutor your children

> *and, if the two of you work well together, it's a good idea to have some effective approaches ready.*
>
> *Just because the actualization of their potential is not dependent upon your teaching them or pulling or coaxing it from them, that doesn't mean that you can't be an important player on the instructional team, if you so wish.*

Let's look at some key elements or approaches for you to remember when working with your children.

KEY ELEMENTS OR APPROACHES

1. Always keep in mind the emerging skills philosophy and the techniques of encouragement, following their lead, and positive redirection.

2. Watch for better and worse times of day, physical environments, and lengths of sessions to work with your children.

3. The medium is the message: If we are feeling anger, we will probably teach more about anger than about math; if we are feeling anxious and hurried, we will probably teach more about anxiety and impatience than about reading. Whenever possible, avoid teaching/tutoring when you really aren't in the mood.

4. Find their ideal balance between success and frustration (at what point they are most motivated) and make an effort to try and balance instruction at that point (this *point* may change from time to time).

5. Attempt to incorporate different subject areas (such as physical coordination, math, or reading) into their areas of interest. (If your children are really into bugs and spiders, and need some extra help with vowel sounds, then work on vowel sounds with bug and spider names.)

6. Make every effort to end tutoring/teaching sessions on a positive note. The last few moments of an activity or experience tend to be remembered best. Children who have a great time reading

with Mom or Dad for 30 minutes, but experience boredom and frustration in the last five minutes will tend to remember the entire experience as boring and frustrating; children who experience a mild degree of boredom or frustration while reading with Mom or Dad for 30 minutes, but really enjoy the last five minutes, will tend to remember the experience more positively.

7. Some helpful techniques might include the Pepsi break, make it a game, my turn—your turn, open-ended and varied questions.

1. Always keep in mind the emerging skills philosophy and the techniques of encouragement, following their lead, and positive redirection.

During the times in which you are playing and working with your children, trying to teach them, helping them learn or practicing an emerging skill, always keep in mind that where they are—their present level of performance or achievement—is just where they're supposed to be. In an hour, or a day, or a month, they may know more or be able to do something better, but right now this is where they are. For example:

If your three-year-olds are "writing" letters, and it appears in your eyes that they are merely stringing together a series of indecipherable squiggles and just pretending to write, remember your emerging skills philosophy: They are writing, in an emerging way. *Keep this philosophy in mind and enjoy the beauty and wonder of their curiosity and desire to communicate through writing. If you want to assist them to write in a more conventional way, the way grown ups do, be sure to be cautious and patient. Move in small steps and let their curiosity lead you. If they think you are correcting them too much, or they are wrong, or their work is not acceptable, your efforts to spur on new learning may well seem like put-downs, and might discourage them from continuing their game (writing).*

Do everything you can to encourage their activity: Comment on how good it feels to be written to, how mature their writing is, how good they must feel writing such a long letter, what a long time they've been working, and so on.

If they provide an opening for you to instruct them in formal letter formation, or ask, "How do you spell_____?" or say,

"You write me a letter now," great! *Jump right in and join the game. Have a ball as you teach/tutor all you like; they asked for it!*

When your seven-year-olds are sitting down doing homework and they throw their papers on the floor and say, "I just don't get it. This ones and tens stuff stinks!" don't forget that many types of learning are not easy, and that failure and frustration often precede success and exaltation. Just by your being there beside them, as a caring person, you are supporting them. Rather than pushing them with statements like "Oh, it's not that hard" or, "Let me show you, I'll do it for you," try to encourage them with comments like "You seem to be working on some real hard stuff there," or, "It looks like you're going to be learning a lot this year!"

Many parents are tempted to solve problems for their children, or in some way make their children's responsibilities or jobs easier, or perhaps blame them for not getting it or working harder. These approaches don't work nearly as well as merely staying nearby, being available when called on, subtly reinforcing positive attempts, and answering questions when asked.

2. Watch for better and worse times of day, physical environments, and lengths of sessions to work with your children.

DIURNAL RHYTHMS

Most individuals have certain times of the day when they are more capable or less capable of performing certain tasks, certain times of day when their energy and awareness levels tend to rise and fall, certain times of day when they are inclined to experience different moods, attitudes, or feelings. These are called *diurnal rhythms*. These rhythms are often subtle and for most people, have only a minor effect and need not dominate how they live their lives, but they are interesting to observe and be aware of. However, some children and adults are more affected by these rhythms. If your children fall into this more affected group, merely becoming aware of their rhythms can help you in your interactions with them and in helping set up daily schedules. Examples:

My nine-year-old daughter has no interest at all in doing any-thing academically related between the hours of 3:30 to 5:00 P.M. (right after school), but she likes to do her homework before dinner (5:00 or 5:15 to 6:30 P.M.) and loves sitting or lying down with my wife or me during the time right before bed, to read, tell stories, and play games. Once lying in her bed, with the lights dimmed, she'd love to spend an hour or two every night reading, going over spelling words, or computing math problems. The discovery of these truths has helped my daugh-ter, wife, and me design more efficient and joyous household schedules and routines.

• •

I love playing music very early in the morning and very late at night, but am rarely interested between 8:00 A.M. and 9:00 P.M. I love exercising between 8:00 A.M. and 6:00 P.M., but hate very early morning and evening workouts. I love to read in the after-noon and early evening, but have too much energy for sitting and reading in the morning, and I fall asleep when I try to read later in the evening. It has taken me years of self-observation and -evaluation to figure these details out, but now that I have, I am much more settled than ever before and much more effi-cient at using the 24 hours each day provides me.

Most elementary classroom teachers find that their stu-dents have more energy and attention for math, reading, and writing in the mornings, and plan those activities at those times. Right before lunch, most teachers place far fewer mental demands on their students, knowing that many are hungry and a bit tired. When children come back to the classroom after lunch and recess, most teachers spend at least a few minutes in quiet, calming, settling-down activities. Experience has taught them that most students need this little buffer zone or calm-down time before they are ready to put their thinking caps back on.

Parents can help their children watch for their own pat-terns in this way, and no doubt help them and themselves become much more efficient in their use of time.

Consider the following 24-hour schedule. If you're the type of person who feels comfortable writing in a book (I, per-sonally, enjoy marking in books that belong to me. I circle ideas I want to remember, write comments, fold pages over instead of using book markers. My wife, on the other hand, treats books as if they were fine works of art, to be saved and protected for eternity. My feeling is that this book belongs to you—unless you checked it out from the library or borrowed it—so you should be allowed to write in it!) I recommend that you fill out the schedule as it relates to you and your diurnal rhythms. After figuring yourself out, you'll be better able to analyze your children.

TIME OF DAY	PREFERRED ACTIVITIES	CHALLENGING/LESS PREFERRED ACTIVITIES
6–7 A.M.		
7–8 A.M.		
8–9 A.M.		
9–10 A.M.		
10–11 A.M.		
11 A.M.–12 P.M.		
12 P.M.–1 P.M.		
1–2 P.M.		
2–3 P.M.		
3–4 P.M.		
4–5 P.M.		
5–6 P.M.		
6–7 P.M.		
7–8 P.M.		
8–9 P.M.		
9–10 P.M.		
10–11 P.M.		
11 P.M.–12 A.M.		
12 A.M.–1 A.M.		
1–2 A.M.		
2–3 A.M.		
3–4 A.M.		
4–5 A.M.		
5–6 A.M.		

YOUR INTERNAL CLOCK (DIURNAL RHYTHMS)

No need to rush on and read the next section. Put some thought into your own personal rhythms. Do you listen to them? Do you set yourself up for success? Fill out a chart like this one as it relates to your children, and then think about it. Are you helping them to understand themselves and take the greatest advantage of their personal rhythms? Now move on to the next section.

PHYSICAL ENVIRONMENTS

In addition to diurnal rhythms, the performance of many children and adults is also significantly affected by the physical conditions that surround them; they do better or less well in certain environments (indoors versus outdoors, warm versus cold rooms, stronger/brighter versus dimmer lights, loose versus more tight-fitting clothes, wearing cotton versus synthetic fabrics, sitting on a hard surface versus a soft one, and so on). Most individuals can adapt fairly well to any and all of these conditions but for others, the physical environment can significantly help or hinder their ability to focus and sustain attention and perform certain tasks.

Some individuals are allergic to certain fabrics and annoyed by the feeling or sensations of others. The clothes they wear can bother and irritate them and have a negative impact on their performance.

Certain people become lethargic and tired whenever they are in their bedrooms, or reclining, or in too warm a room, or after a big meal, or when the lights are very dim. For these fortunate or unfortunate individuals, studying or reading under any of these conditions is an invitation for a nap, rather than productive activity.

On beautiful, warm days many of my college students ask if I will hold class outside on the lawn. I used to try this once in awhile, but, no more! I have found that while most college students are able to pay attention and participate just as well outside as in the classroom, a certain percentage, perhaps 10 to 20 percent (this is not a research-based approximation, but a subjective, unreliable guess!) are so distracted by the physical sensations of being outdoors on a beautiful day that they gain almost nothing from the class.

Once again, on a personal note, I have spent many years evaluating physical environments in which I study and learn more and less efficiently. Any or all of the following conditions can lower my ability to think, attend, and learn.

• •

clothing labels that touch my skin
wearing wool
sitting on a seat that is too hard
reading or studying while reclining
background music or noise
tight-fitting clothes or shoes
a lot of action or activity around me
strong odors in the air
not enough light

• •

I don't know how much is due to heredity and how much to modeling on me, but I do know that my daughter's reactions are similar to mine in many of the sensitivities described in the above list. This knowledge is helping all of us—my wife, my daughter, and me—establish environments that are more conducive to Rachel's comfort, learning, and success.

Under what conditions do your children prefer to work, and work best? In what room or environment, wearing what types of clothing, with what types of background noises or sounds (have you noticed the recent proliferation of audiotapes that play continuous sounds of nature, such as birds, breaking waves, and wind through trees?) under what types of lighting, seated in what positions, on what firmness of surface? All of these questions, and their answers, can assist parents in setting up optimal learning environments.

Don't think for a moment that your children learn just like you. It may be true, but it may not be. Observe and discuss these issues with your children. I remind you, and myself, that knowledge is power and self-awareness is the first step to positive change. *People/children do not all learn in the same way or study best in the same environments.*

Look over the following list, evaluate yourself, and determine which environments affect you and what their effects are. Once again, I ask that you please not rush. The parents who learn the most from this book are not the ones who read it the fastest; they are the ones who thoughtfully apply the ideas to themselves and their children. Now that you've been warned, look at the list.

Consider how each of the following environmental stimuli would probably affect your ability to perform various activities (such as relaxing, playing, reading, writing, carrying on a conversation).

warm room	neon lights
cold room	fluorescent lights
wearing cotton	quiet environment
wearing polyester	music or speech around you
wearing wool	sitting on a hard surface
wearing (other fabrics)	sitting on a soft surface
tight clothing	reclining
loose clothing	others in the room
no clothing at all	in the room alone
labels touching your skin	other:_____
bright lights	other:_____
dim lights	other:_____

Now that you've thought about these issues as they relate to you, go back and look at them as they relate to your children. Please do consider sitting down with your children and asking them their opinions. See what they have to say. (If their response is, "Ga, ga, goo, goo, Mama, Dada," then I probably should have mentioned that discussing this with infants and young toddlers may not be appropriate. Sorry.)

LENGTHS OF SESSIONS

Do your children prefer to work for short periods of time and move around a bit before continuing an activity, or do they like to just start and finish, with no breaks? For how long can they concentrate and remain productive? Does this vary depending on the activity or time of day? This is important knowledge to possess and to help them understand. This knowledge should play a critical role in determining the books you read together, the activities you involve them in, the toys and games you buy them, and, when they enter kindergarten or first grade, and begin having homework, their study schedules.

3. The medium is the message.

If we are feeling anger we will probably teach more about anger than about math; if we are feeling anxious and hurried we will probably teach more about anxiety and impatience than about reading. Whenever possible, avoid teaching/tutoring when you really aren't in the mood.

Have you ever become upset, or impatient, or perhaps bored when trying to teach your children something, but you kept up with it anyway? (If your answer to this question is "no," then you're either an incredibly patient and together person, or you're not being honest with yourself, or you need to lower your medication and get back to earth!) I have. The unfortunate part of this is that very often the attitude that we have while teaching or tutoring has a more lasting impact on our children than the subject matter we are trying to convey. In general, it's a much better idea, once one of these negative emotions begins to arise, to change direction. Either move on to a different topic, or make what you're doing more fun, or stop and discuss the feelings you're having and deal with them. The worst thing to do is let the feelings boil and fester, and try to continue the session. For example:

Parent to two-year-old: "You asked me to read you this book and I'm going to and you're going to listen. Now stop that looking around and complaining and look at the pictures!"

• •

Mom working with her six-year-old on math problems: "Now just stop being such a smart aleck and do these problems the way I showed you!"

• •

Dad building a sand castle at the beach with his four-year-old: "I don't care if you don't want to play anymore; we started building this sand castle together and we're going to finish it together!"

Parent to an eight-year-old who is being made to write thank-you notes for birthday presents: "You're driving me crazy. If you ever want to have another party, you'd better get to work and finish these thank-you notes!"

What kind of message are these children getting? What is the experience teaching them?

- Having my parents read to me is great? No! They get so grouchy just because I get bored—I hate it when they read to me.

- Math with Mom is fun? No! Math isn't fun and neither is Mom.

- Building sand castles with Daddy is a great way to spend a vacation? No! The messages are: You finish whatever you start even if you don't like it, and vacations on the beach can be difficult and stressful!

- Writing thank-you notes is rewarding? No! It's hardly worth having a party if you have to go through all this hassle and anxiety after it's over.

The medium is the message. *How* we say things is often more important than *what* we say. Our attitudes toward things are often more important than our actions.

Sometimes it's very hard to hide our feelings and thoughts from our loved ones; therefore,

● ●

parents who hate math should be very cautious about tutoring their children in math.

parents who are in a rush and don't really have the time to spend reading a story, or finishing a puzzle, or playing a game with their children should tell that to their children and continue the activity when they are able to really focus on it.

parents who are in a bad mood should deal with their emotions/mood—perhaps discuss it with others in the family—prior to assisting their children with their schoolwork or projects.

● ●

4. Find the ideal balance between success and frustration (at what point are your children most motivated); make an effort to try and balance instruction at that point.

Important points bear repeating. Let's look once again at the question of how difficult or challenging activities should be. This topic was discussed earlier, (Chapter 2), as it related to encouragement. Now the subject is success versus frustration and failure.

While the following percentages are only a rough guideline and vary from child to child and from situation to situation, educators usually conceptualize learning tasks as follows.

- *Independent level.* A child is able to perform successfully at approximately the 85 to 90+ percent level— very few errors and little stumbling over not quite mastered skills—with no assistance.

- *Instructional level.* A child is able to perform successfully at approximately the 75 to 85 percent level— some errors and stumbling over not quite mastered skills—however, assistance to correct errors and provide instruction is readily available.

- *Frustration level.* A child is able to perform successfully below the 70 to 75 percent level—this is regarded as too difficult, too frustrating for most children, even if assistance is readily available.

These percentages vary with different children. Those who have had a history of failure, or aren't very confident, or aren't as motivated to learn, need to experience more success. The percentages listed above need to be higher to keep them motivated, feeling good, and on task. On the opposite extreme, children who are quite motivated, confident, or very persistent, can often handle more difficult materials or tasks than the listed percentages would indicate. Watch your children when they're working and be sensitive to the cues they're providing you. They'll let you know, in some way, if the material is too hard, too easy, or just right. Look at these examples:

You're practicing the names of animals with animal flash cards, and your children are only getting half of the names correct, with lots of guessing and mistakes. They are becoming frustrated and want to stop playing. The next time you or they want to practice those flash cards, include only some of the harder animals, and all of the easier ones. Stack the deck so they can get 85+ percent correct. They'll learn more, be less frustrated, and want to play longer.

. . . .

Most five-year-olds will have more fun, experience more success, and improve their skills faster and better if they play frisbee from 10 feet away and 85+ percent of the throws are thrown and caught well, rather than from 20 feet away with only 50 percent success.

. . . .

If you're reading a book to three-year-olds and find that it's a struggle to keep their attention, perhaps the book is too long, or doesn't have enough pictures, or the vocabulary is too difficult. If their attention is excellent, and they keep asking for more books, or for you to expand upon details in the story ("Why did the bunny run away?" or "How could you make a house out of straw, without wood and nails?" or "Is that the same kind of bear we have in our zoo?") perhaps they're ready for some higher-level books, with more difficult vocabulary and more detail.

. . . .

Seven- and eight-year-olds who struggle every week to get 70 to 75 percent on their Friday spelling tests despite studying their words every night may have too many words, or the words may be too hard. (Talk to their teachers!) However, if they can correctly and consistently spell 90 to 100 percent of their words when they come home for the first time, expand their list; have them practice other, related words, and perhaps words of their own selection. (Also, talk to their teachers and let them know that the words are too easy for your children, and you'd like to challenge them a bit more.)

A little challenge, a little frustration, a little tension in learning is good. It ensures that the tasks or materials are not too easy, and your children are pushing themselves a bit. While 100 percents and A+s aren't bad, if we only have our children working at tasks they have already mastered, there probably isn't a lot of new learning going on and they aren't getting the most out of their time or potential.

Sometimes children and adults need to relax, take it easy, and enjoy the successful feelings that can accompany doing things that are easy; however, if too much time is spent involved in activities like this, growth and new levels of achievement can be stifled.

Now, before moving on to the next section, a quick, little quiz. Don't look back after you read the following questions. Read them, look away from the book for a minute, and think. The questions:

1. What are the corresponding percentages for the independent, instructional, and frustration levels just described?

2. Why is it important to keep these percentages in mind?

3. How and why might these percentages be higher or lower for certain children?

How did you do on your quiz? Well, I hope. If not, you may wish to reread the last few pages.

5. Attempt to incorporate different subject areas into topics that are of interest to your children.

Your four-year-olds love to play with your costume jewelry. You want to work with them on counting and sorting objects by different characteristics (such as color, size, and shape). Why not use the jewelry for some math games (for example, line up the rings by size, or count the bracelets, or put the necklaces in order, from shortest to longest)?

Your six-year-olds have a vast collection of toy figures (soldiers, farm animals, assorted creatures). You want to work with them on letter sounds and spelling. Why not make up names for each of the figures, write them out on cards, and then match the figures to the cards?

Your eight-year-olds love rap music. You want to work with them on soccer skills (such as kicking and bouncing a soccer ball off different body parts). Why not turn on some rap music,

> *grab a soccer ball, and kick and bounce the ball back and forth to one another to the rhythm of the music?*

The idea here is to start with something that interests and motivates them, then think of a way to use that to get them involved in other activities.

This approach provides you with excellent opportunities to use your own creativity, while, at the same time, encouraging new learning and practice for your children in various other areas.

6. Make every effort to end tutoring/teaching sessions with at least two or three positive minutes.

Here are two often-heard sayings, both of which are very relevant to working with our children.

1. Too much of a good thing is no good!

2. End on a positive note.

The critical point here is that we all, children and adults, tend to remember the last few moments of an experience—how it ended—more potently and clearly than any other part. Think about it. Think about someone you used to date, or your most recent vacation, or the last time you tried to teach your children something. One of the first things you'll remember is probably the last part of the experience—how it ended. Odds are that the feelings you associate with that old boyfriend or girlfriend, or your most recent vacation, or the last time you tried to teach your children something, are those you felt near the end of the experience. That's how the mind tends to work—not always, but there is a tendency for the mind to work in this way.

Now, think about going outside and playing kickball or catch with your son or daughter, or working on flash cards with them, or sitting down to help them or listen to them practice their math facts or ABCs. Think about it, and burn into your mind that you want it to end positively. Remind yourself to end the experience while it's still going well, before boredom sets in or attention starts dwindling. Promise yourself that if things aren't going well, you'll in someway simplify, or spice up, or energize the activity and end it on a more positive note.

The next time you say to your son, "How about reading some books together?" you want him to think, "Books. Reading with Dad. Oh yeah, I remember. The last time we did that he told me this really neat story after we read for awhile." That's what you want him to remember, rather than, "Books. Reading with Dad. Oh yeah, I remember. The last time we did that he got mad because I wanted to stop. I just got tired and he wanted to go on and on and on. No, I don't think I want to go through that again!"

Remember the curve from Chapter 4:

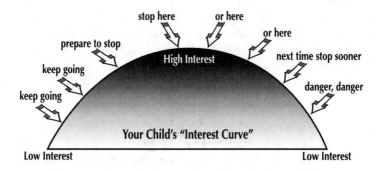

Remember and put this knowledge into practice—end on a positive note.

7. Some helpful techniques: the Pepsi Break, make it a game, my turn—your turn, open-end and varied questions.

THE PEPSI BREAK

Whether you call it a Pepsi Break, a Coke Break, or just Take A Break, the technique here is the same: Take a deep breath of air and wait a few seconds before responding to questions, asking questions, or intervening. The reasoning behind this is that we adults, far too often (1) answer questions our children can answer themselves; (2) ask questions too hurriedly and unclearly, and (3) act or respond without thinking, and then have to reverse our original actions and responses.

Taking a deep breath and waiting for just a few seconds not only leads to our having more fully functioning brains (our brains work much better when supplied with oxygen), but also can lead to providing our children with enough time to answer their own questions and make their own decisions. Breathing also gives us the opportunity to carefully consider requests we plan on making and questions we intend to verbalize and grants us an extra moment to think about how we wish to respond to certain behavior.

Some situations may require that we take two or three or four Pepsi Breaks (deep breaths) before deciding what to do or say, or how to respond (when your four-year-old daughter asks, "Mommy, do you and Daddy have sex together?" or your eight-year-old son says, "I want to get my ears pierced just like Johnnie's, can we do it this weekend?"). That's fine. It's better to wait awhile and do or say the right thing or ask the question, in a clear way, the first time, rather than make a mistake and have to reverse ourselves or restate something.

MAKE IT A GAME

Most children like to play games and are much more willing to work or study if the format is fun and motivating.

Simply throwing a ball back and forth to Mom or Dad is fun but counting how many times you can do it without dropping it, or having a target contest, or trying to knock over a line of tin cans can be a lot of fun!

Reading a book to Mom or Dad is okay, but taking turns, using different voices, and pretending to be the characters in the story can be really exciting.

Working on math flash cards is good practice but pretending that every flash card correctly answered is another train car attached to the train engine, and seeing how long the train can get, is a real blast!

Whenever you or your children can think of a way to practice a skill in a fun and different way, do it. Not only will they be more motivated to stay involved in the activity, but they'll also tend to stay involved longer. Added to this is the good feelings and attitude they'll associate with the activity and the extra practice you'll both have using your creativity.

MY TURN—YOUR TURN

A quick and easy way to change the pace while working with your children, and also bring some extra fun and variety in, is to take turns. You read a sentence, I read a sentence; I kick the ball, you kick the ball; you draw for 15 seconds, I draw for 15 seconds; I think of someone and you have 20 questions to guess who it is, you think of someone and I have 20 questions to guess who it is; I'll test you on five spelling words—then you test me on five. Taking turns like this makes the time with your children more of a mutual, shared experience, and less of an I teach, you learn practice session. It also gives them the opportunity to work cooperatively with another person and involves them in a wider variety of skills (such as reading *and* listening while being read to; kicking *and* pitching the ball to the kicker; drawing *and* sharing a creative experience; asking questions *and* answering them).

You can either begin by taking turns, or use the technique to energize or enliven an activity that is beginning to turn tedious or boring.

OPEN-END AND VARIED QUESTIONS

One final technique relates to the types of questions we ask our children. Hopefully we want and expect them to have both the ability to come up with *the* right answer when there is *a* right answer, to expand on answers and express thoughts and feelings, to memorize facts, and to think. In order to help them do this we need to vary the type and level of questions we ask.

Closed or *closed-end questions* yield short, to-the-point answers.

• •

Who was the first president of the United States?

Do you want to go to McDonald's for dinner?

What color do you get when you mix yellow and red?

What sound do the letters "sh" make?

• •

There's nothing wrong with *closed* questions; they have their place in teaching, learning, and life. We just need to make sure that these are not the only types of questions we ask our children.

Open or *open-end questions* allow children to think more, and come up with more original and often longer answers.

• •

If Washington had been made the king of America, instead of the first president of the United States, how might our country be different today?

Why do you like McDonald's so much?

What colors do you think look good together? What combinations don't you like?

Let's see how many words we can think of that start with the "sh" sound.

• •

Another aspect of questioning is the level or type of thinking that is required of the person being questioned. The lowest level of questioning focuses on facts—have you memorized or do you know *x, y, z?*

• •

What was the name of the girl in the story?

What materials did the boys use to make the wagon?

What kind of dog is that?

• •

Parents (and teachers) are usually very adept at asking this type of question, so adept that the vast majority of questions put to children are at this level. Now, just as in the case with closed questions, basic knowledge/factual questions have a place in teaching and learning. They have a place, but should not dominate our goals or our interactions with our children. There's a lot more to knowledge and learning than memorizing facts! Beginning when most children are about three or four years old, parents can and should begin focusing more on higher-level questions.

Higher-level questions are usually *open end* and require children to demonstrate that they understand something, rather than simply have memorized it, are able to use and apply their understanding to other situations, analyze information, compare and contrast, relate new learning to old learning, and evaluate problems. Higher level questions make children think more.

• •

How do you think the girl in the story felt when her mother left? Why?

In what ways was the wagon the boys made like your wagon? In what ways was it different?

What do you think that breed of dogs was bred for? Why?

• •

Before phrasing a question, ask yourself: Do I want to see if they have memorized the material correctly, or understand it, or can relate this knowledge to other knowledge? Hopefully you will decide to vary your questions more, to place less emphasis on pure memorization, more on understanding, and still more on higher-level thinking skills such as analyzing and pulling various types and bits and pieces of knowledge together. And yes, I was serious when I said this is appropriate for three-year-olds.

RECOMMENDATIONS

1. Whether or not you focus your energies on teaching and tutoring your children, you *are* their teacher and tutor. Setting up a rich environment that allows and encourages them to explore and experience is the most critical role you play as a teacher/tutor.

2. By being productive, verbal, investigative, literate, and intelligent individuals we are serving as excellent models for our children's development of their own productivity, verbal skills, investigative nature, literacy, and intelligence.

3. Know your children and help them learn to know themselves. If you and they are aware of the times of day when they perform different activities better and less well, physical environments in which they are able and less able to think and learn, and how long they can perform different tasks without overtaxing themselves, both their teaching and learning and yours will be enhanced.

4. The medium is the message—be reminded that the feeling or atmosphere that exists while you are working with your children has a tremendous effect on what they learn. The best time to work with them is when you're both in the mood for it; the best subjects in which to work with them are those toward which you have a good attitude. (If you just mumbled, "Then we'll never be working together!" you need to reread this chapter and really think of ways to motivate your children, and make working and playing together a more enjoyable experience.)

5. Discover how much challenge and how much failure your children can handle and still feel successful. Attempt to orchestrate their new learning at a level that provides them with some challenge but is not so difficult or frustrating that they will be discouraged (75+ percent success rate at a minimum).

6. Start with their interest areas and incorporate subjects or topics into those areas in which *you want to work with them.* Children are usually much more motivated to work with you in a given subject if you incorporate their interests or hobbies.

7. Hopefully all your teaching and learning with your children will flow productively and joyously, but if it doesn't, make a special effort to end sessions on a positive note. It is the last few minutes of working with you that will remain most vividly in their memories.

8. Take a deep breath and think before you help your children, ask a question, respond to a behavior, or make a request.

9. Whenever possible, make your teaching/tutoring sessions fun. Kids love to play games and most topics can be translated into dozens or hundreds of different game formats.

10. Most children enjoy taking turns. One game that you can use to enliven your interactions with your children is "my turn—your turn."

11. Watch how you word your questions. Make an effort to ask far more *open* questions than *closed,* and to concentrate more on questions that make your children think, rather than on questions that merely require them to remember something or simply understand.

SUMMARY

Parents don't have to be the ones to formally teach their children to read, multiply, play soccer, or learn the scales on the piano. They don't have to be key members of the teaching + learning team—but most often are.

To function well on this teaching + learning team, to be good teachers/tutors of their children, parents need to focus on a number of key skills. While not a comprehensive guide to working with your children, this chapter has described a number of techniques to help parents in this role.

CHAPTER 10

CONSISTENCY

INTRODUCTION

H ow important is it that your children's school and home learning environments are consistent? If there are a number of teachers/tutors/role models at home (more than one parent, a grandparent, or older siblings), how important is it that they interact with your young learners in similar ways? How important is it that the people who influence your children—parents, teachers, and other role models—be consistent in their responses to achievements and frustrations, challenges and low motivation periods? These questions will all be addressed in this chapter.

THE RELEVANCE OF CONSISTENCY IN THE CONTEXT OF THIS BOOK

This topic, consistency, is of greater importance in the encouragement of potential than in other areas of learning because such a significant part of the maximization of potential is dependent on psychological and social factors. Most children do at least all right in their area(s) of potential, but many of them slide along on their innate ability, and never come near to tapping the aptitude they actually possess.

If we, the significant adults in children's lives, really wish to assist them in optimizing their ability, we need to pay particular attention to how they interact in a variety of settings. We need to try to enhance their learning and motivation in as many ways as possible— consistency being one of those ways.

Most children can function quite well moving back and forth between systems with different rules, expectations, and standards. They learn what is acceptable and unacceptable behavior in varying settings, and with short periods of trial-and-error, adjust their behaviors. No big problem. Some settings may not be ideal; others are. Some settings may see children in a different light, focus on different behavior and learning goals, or be less or more consistent, but, in general, children are adaptable enough to deal with these inconsistencies and variations.

This is not quite so true when discussing individuals' areas of particular strength, or potential. Many a fine artist, athlete, and scholar have been lost to the world because of one bad teacher, or a critical sibling or parent. Hundreds of thousands of possible Mozarts, van Goghs, Chris Everts, Lee Iaccocas, Hemingways, and Oprahs have turned their backs on their potentials and opted for jobs and careers that did not allow them to share the beauty and brilliance they possessed. Not always, but sometimes, these losses have been due to being the victims of environments that did not nourish and inspire them, environments that were inconsistent with what they needed to bring out the best in themselves.

The message that this chapter should convey is that yes, consistency (whenever possible) is desirable; yes, we should convince teachers, spouses, other relatives, and siblings to interact in similar ways with our children, in their individual areas of potential. For many, or perhaps most children, this is not critical or necessary, but for some it is, and therefore it is the most desirable route to follow. Three examples should help to explain.

Jessica and Pam are unknown to each other and living hundreds of miles apart. They are both five-year-olds and both have the innate potential to be outstanding soccer players. Both girls can run like the wind, kick a ball with incredible speed and accuracy with either foot, regain their equilibrium in midair, and are dynamos of near limitless energy. Their parents have enrolled them in soccer clinics and play with them whenever time is available. That's the end of the similarities. Now for a couple of critical differences.

Jessica is in a kindergarten where her teacher highly values her physical skills, and allows her to move around a lot and incorporate motor movement in new learning, whenever possible. Pam's teacher believes that five-year-olds need to learn to sit quietly and listen, and spend extended periods of time concentrating on memorizing numbers and letters.

Jessica's teacher is constantly praising her young athlete regarding her physical gifts. Pam is constantly sent to the time-out corner for moving around too much, and is often referred to as "a little jumping bean," "hyperactive," and "the little miss can't stay in her seat."

When both girls enter first grade, Jessica decides to continue her soccer and join a team, and she continues to find abundant support for her skills and self-fulfillment playing soccer. Pam, on the other hand, becomes more and more of a behavior problem and decides that she doesn't want to play soccer anymore.

Was consistency an issue here? Did Jessica, who will now possess one more area of excellence in her life, and may perhaps someday be recognized for her achievement by having the joy of participating on a winning team, or perhaps receiving a college scholarship, or even an opportunity to play in the World Cup or Olympics, benefit from a school environment that supported her potential, and was consistent with the values supported in her home? Yes! Was the inconsistency and lack of support experienced by Pam related to her dropping out of soccer, and possibly turning her back forever on an area of significant potential? Maybe—I believe it was.

You may be thinking that this is too simplistic. Perhaps you think, "If that one teacher was able to turn her off from soccer she probably would have given up later down the line anyway." Maybe, but maybe not. Most of us can think back to turning points in our lives, places or times where we had a choice—go this way or that—when we made a decision. Some of us remember that point fondly, joyously full of thanks that it led us to a place where we wanted to go; others look back at that point (or those points) with regret and thoughts of, "had I only…"

Here is another story, other children to illustrate the possible importance of consistency.

Bradley and Dave don't know each other, but they share something very unique in common. Both are eight-year-olds, living in different parts of the country; both have potential in the area of design (drawing, three dimensional visualization, sensitivity to shape and color). Both boys have the potential to be architects, or builders, artists, or decorators. As you might have guessed, one of them is about to face a consistently supportive environment in his ninth year of life, while the other is going to face a significant roadblock.

Both boys have mothers, siblings, relatives, and teachers who are aware of their abilities, make every effort to encourage and support them, and take great pride in the obvious skills they possess.

Now, here it comes, one of these boys is about to face an inconsistency, a significant roadblock to the encouragement of his potential.

Bradley's dad is very pleased about his son's abilities. He has taken him to art shows, has bought him his own camera, has framed and hung his son's artwork on his office walls, and has begun a special college account so that in ten years Bradley will be able to attend the college of his choice, to enable him to progress as far as possible in the career—perhaps design-oriented—that he chooses.

Dave's dad—the inconsistent ingredient in the consistency formula that this chapter is recommending—has put up with his son's artsy-craftsy stuff until now, but has become impatient with Dave's lack of interest in sports and physical activities, and concerned about "an eight-year-old kid, who should be out there roughin' it up, but just sits around drawing all the time." The dad has recently become verbally critical of his son's expenditure of time and told him that it's time to pick a sport (hopefully football—Dad's sport) and start getting involved in that. Dave's dad has decided that he doesn't want to pay for all the extra art and design classes they've been sending Dave to, and a number of heated arguments have arisen lately over Mom's encouragement of Dave's involvement in all this sissy stuff.

Can Dave still become a competent, confident, and happy architect or builder or artist or decorator? Of course! Will his father's resistance be an inhibiting factor? I think so! Would Dave have a better chance of realizing his potential and feeling good about himself and his abilities if his dad were less against it, or perhaps even supportive? My guess is yes. What's yours?

Now here's another example.

> *Brandy and Rhonda are both seven years old. In many ways they are very different. One is tall; the other is short. One has two siblings; the other has none. One has white skin; the other has brown. One lives in Florida; the other lives in Arizona. Many differences, but also many similarities. They both come from single-parent families where a mother is raising them with minimal assistance from other adults. They are both deeply loved and beautifully cared for. And they both have significant potential in the area of mathematics.*
>
> *Now for the most critical difference that may have an impact on their area of greatest potential—mathematics. Brandy goes to a school where all children of the same age work on the same math concepts, at the same time, and are not allowed or encouraged to learn or achieve beyond the group. Added to this, Brandy's teachers all share the view that math is basically a boys' subject, and girls should look to other areas for achievement, self-expression, and success. Rhonda, on the other hand, is in a school where children are allowed to advance at their own speed in all subjects, and are provided with enriching and fun ways to apply their knowledge and skills in different subject areas to real-life situations. Also, at Rhonda's school the predominant attitude is that, as far as success in any endeavor, individual ability and motivation are critical, not sex, race, or any other characteristic.*

My crystal ball tells me that one of these girls has a far better chance of success in a math-oriented career, while the other will be far less likely to pursue a career that relies on mathematical skills.

Now for the questions.

1. Which girl will be more likely to go into a career in a math-oriented field?

   a. Rhonda
   b. Brandy   (Answer: a)

2. The most critical reason(s) that Rhonda will probably go further in math is (are):

   a. height
   b. number of siblings
   c. school curriculum
   d. sexism (discrimination because of sex)
   e. answers c and d   (Answer: e)

I propose that Rhonda has a much higher likelihood of advanced achievement in mathematics, and that the two most critical reasons are her school's curriculum and the attitudes of her teachers. Congratulations Rhonda.

I propose that Brandy's two biggest roadblocks to advanced achievement in mathematics are her school's curriculum and the attitudes of her teachers (sexism).

I further propose that the most important thing Brandy's mother can do to help her daughter maximize her potential in math is to share her concerns with the teacher and principal, and if that doesn't work, move her to a new classroom, or, in this case, probably to a different school. "How radical!" you may be thinking. Darn right it's radical! But, look at the choices here. Brandy is almost certainly not, I repeat not, going to go as far as she might in math if something isn't done to correct the situation. This waste of potential may well occur despite all the love and caring her mother is going to provide. Does this sound right or fair? No, it doesn't. Yet this situation will not correct itself unless Brandy's mom does something. She must act!

Some people are incredibly resilient and are able to stand even taller and stronger in the face of adversity, but most of us aren't and don't. Most of us like, and some of us need, our environments to be more consistently helpful and reinforcing. When parents find their children to be in environments that are not consistently helpful, nurturing, and reinforcing, they should and must act to change those environments.

RECOMMENDATIONS

1. Talk to key people who interact with you and your children and express to them your desire to reinforce, and have *them* reinforce, your children's areas of potential. Try to enlist their support.

2. If you and your partner can't come to an agreement about the importance of nurturing your children's potential, seek professional help—perhaps a counselor or psychologist—to assist you in working out your differences.

3. When you observe other individuals saying or doing something that encourages your children's areas of potential, thank and encourage them. (Praise and encourage the praiser/encourager.)

4. Take charge!

SUMMARY

Potential, an incredible gift, but, unfortunately, a gift that is rarely taken full advantage of. Many children manage to extract much of their potential despite having to interact with various types of people who do not encourage them, but, for some, even small amounts of criticism or disapproval can be devastating. It therefore is recommended that parents make every effort to encourage their children's areas of potential by surrounding them with individuals who will be supportive, individuals who will help and encourage children to be all they can be.

CHAPTER 11

GROUPS AT RISK OF NOT REALIZING THEIR POTENTIAL

INTRODUCTION

A ll that you have learned in the past ten chapters will help you in your quest to encourage potential in your children; however, a bit more needs to be said about certain groups at risk of not realizing their potential. The following pages will point out some special considerations that parents are advised to keep in mind when raising children who fall into one or more of the following groups.

● ●

females
gifted
learning disabled (LD)
attention-deficit/hyperactivity disorders (ADHD)
mentally retarded (MR)/developmentally disabled (DD)
emotionally/behaviorally disordered
sensory and/or physically challenged
culturally and/or linguistically different

● ●

THE RELEVANCE OF GROUPS AT RISK IN THE CONTEXT OF THIS BOOK

Knowledge is power. The more we know about ourselves, our children, teaching, learning, our environment, and our society, the more knowledge we have and the better able we will be to deal with situations as they arise—to make decisions. Many in our society treat females differently than males; schools and the work world are very often more hospitable to good readers and writers than to those with deficits in these areas; people who are blind are challenged in ways very different from those who are emotionally disordered. To be aware of these differences can help parents more effectively structure their children's lives.

Taking a focused look at the groups into which your children may fall should help you bring into greater clarity the specific environmental factors that you must be aware of to maximize their areas of potential.

The purpose of this chapter is not to highlight differences between children, or to criticize society, or to diminish the level of expectations parents can and should have for their children. The purpose here is to describe some of the challenges that certain children may face in their early years. This is being done in order to increase the likelihood that you will notice and be aware if these conditions exist in your children's worlds. Another purpose of this chapter is to provide you with additional approaches to counteract the limiting effects these conditions may have on the realization of your children's potential.

Each of the groups mentioned in the introduction (females, gifted, learning disabled, and others) will be briefly described or defined. The unique challenges they often face in the realization of their potential will be discussed and, finally, recommendations will be made.

Once again, keep in mind that the first ten chapters of this book apply to all children. Children, despite their sex, IQ, disabilities, abilities, or ethnicity are first and foremost children. They are more like all other children their age than they are like adults of their particular group. Children have far more in common with one another than they have differences. Please do keep this in mind.

FEMALES

Who Is Included in this Group?

This group includes all children of the female gender. This is the largest of all at-risk groups that may face special challenges to the realizing of potential.

Challenges to Maximizing Potential

The roles, rights, rewards, and responsibilities of females have changed dramatically in many cultures over the past two or three decades, but equality of the sexes has not yet been achieved. While the horizon of possibilities for females in North America (please keep in mind that this section was written using North America as a reference, and may or may not apply in other areas of the world) has expanded dramatically, and continues to expand, females continue to face familial and societal limitations in education, career choice, income level, and other areas. Some of the causes for these conditions and inequities find their roots in the early childhood years.

While a number of innate, inborn differences exist between males and females, research reveals that familial and societal expectations also play roles in many choices that children make. Most researchers presently believe that familial and societal expectations are more powerful determinants than innate, inborn differences in choices such as

• •

playing with dolls versus building blocks and toys with wheels.

assuming the role of the brave aggressor versus the role of more passive and sensitive bystander.

seeing oneself as an I-can-do! problem solver versus a Help-me!/Save-me/I-need-assistance type of individual.

aspirations to careers in math and science versus working with infants and young children.

interest in bouncing, throwing, and kicking balls versus dance, rhythm, and acrobatics.

experiencing pain, fear, and tears versus holding these emotions in and being "strong" or "tough."

• •

In each of these categories, and many others, there may be small and subtle inborn differences between the sexes, but the more we learn about the power of expectations, early life experiences, and reinforcements/rewards, the more it seems that many of our young female children are being guided in different directions than their male counterparts.

In the majority of children's lives the burden of early upbringing and nurturing falls on the very capable shoulders—not to mention feet, hands, knees, backs, consciousness, and pocketbooks—of their mothers. Mothers are overwhelmingly the primary care providers for all children, male and female; for female children, mothers are by far the most accessible, credible, influential, valued, and important role models.

Think for a moment—how do most people learn to parent and nurture? Where did *you* learn most of what you know about parenting and nurturing? Was it from books? Probably not. From high school or college courses? Very doubtful. From television? Get serious! It was more than likely from your own parents. For females, chances are great that many of their approaches to parenting and nurturing are similar to those of their mothers. Where did your mother learn her skills? Right—from her mother, and so on.

What we're getting at here is that while many in society are making dramatic efforts to change how they perceive the roles of males and females, certain forces, such as where we get the bulk of our early learning about parenting and nurturing, remain rooted in tradition, which is often sadly, but significantly, rooted in sex-role stereotypes.

For the past twenty years one of my favorite questions of children (two to ten years old) has been, "What do you want to do or be when you grow up?" My own personal research tells me that the answers I receive most often from males are different from the most common answers provided by females. Males far less often mention children, marriage, families, and nurturing or artistic careers such as teaching, nursing, and the arts. Females, on the other hand, focus solely on a career role/job far less often than males, and far less often mention careers that involve power over others, huge financial rewards, and physical danger such as president, boss of everyone, doctor, police officer, fire fighter, astronaut. The answers I receive today from females are more varied than a few years ago, but very clearly different than the typical or average boy answer.

What does this all mean? It means that still today, in our age of equal opportunity, affirmative action, and women's liberation/rights, the environments in which most females spend their first few years continue to subtly convey the message that they have more limits than boys, or perhaps that certain roles are more acceptable for them and others less acceptable.

Not always, but far too often, television, parents and grandparents, day-care providers, teachers, and society in general foster these limiting images and perceptions. We parents of daughters need to be aware of this, look for it, and combat it.

RECOMMENDATIONS

1. Awareness is a critical factor in the process of change. Merely making yourself more aware and in tune with subtle sex-role stereotyping will assist you in limiting your daughters' exposures to it. Be aware of the television shows they watch, the books they read and that are read to them, and the attitudes of the providers and teachers who work with them.

2. Search for television shows, books, situations, and individuals who portray and refer to females in ways that you wish your daughters to be exposed to.

3. Make an effort to enhance your daughters' awareness of and exposure to competent, well-balanced, happy, self-realizing, and successful women who occupy challenging, varied, fulfilling, and nontraditional jobs, who are breaking the molds/stereotypes, going their own ways.

4. Monitor your daughters' teachers to be sure that females receive treatment equal to that of males in the classroom. This is especially important in the areas of leadership, mathematics, and science, areas where expectations for females have traditionally been lower than for males.

5. Monitor grade-level testing results in your local school districts. Are females achieving at the same level as males? If not, ask questions; make waves!

6. Be aware of your own values and how you express them to your daughters. Do you perceive women as limited in their abilities, roles, or opportunities? If so, be aware that *who* you are and *what* you believe is influencing who your daughters will become. Accept this truth, or work on changing yourself.

THE GIFTED

Who Is Included in this Group?

The traditional view of giftedness—one that today is regarded as very limited—was that the gifted were those who scored very well on intelligence (IQ) tests. These tests were (I say *were;* however, they are still used by most psychologists and educational systems) supposed to measure individuals' innate potential and ability levels. They were (and are) supposed to measure the ability a child possessed, and this ability was supposed to stand by itself, unaffected by training, education, creativity, or motivation. The tests focused on logical-mathematical and verbal-linguistic abilities. A very high score in mathematical-logical, verbal/linguistic, or the average of the two, determined one's intelligence. Only those who scored very well on these tests, in the top 2 percent or so, were considered gifted. The very highest scorers—far, far fewer than .5 percent—were regarded as geniuses.

Most newer, more progressive views of giftedness broaden this group in two main ways.

1. Today we look at more areas than logical-mathematical and verbal/linguistic abilities.

2. Factors other than test scores are more often considered.

In the more progressive view of giftedness we look at many possible areas, with various theorists proposing more and more areas each year. Besides logical-mathematical and verbal/linguistic, other areas that have been proposed are

• •

musical.

artistic.

spatial (seeing patterns, shapes, designs).

kinesthetic (motor coordination and movement).

interpersonal (understanding others).

intrapersonal (understanding self).

spiritual (understanding one's relationship with God or the cosmos).

naturalist (understanding nature).

culinary (cooking and sensitivity to taste).

● ●

And the list goes on and on.

Interesting, isn't it? Think about it. Think about children and adults you know and have known. Think about all the abilities an individual might possess. There are many facets of human growth and development that lead to many different careers and hobbies. Why should we not consider individuals with extremely high levels of potential in each of these as gifted?

Another part of the new way of looking at giftedness is that there's more to it than innate, inborn potential. Two other ingredients are now proposed as critical in the formula or recipe of giftedness. These are (1) creativity and (2) motivation/drive/task commitment/follow-through.

Now for a quick review. In the newer view of giftedness there are many realms or areas in which to be gifted, and, in each realm or area there are three main ingredients: *ability, creativity,* and *motivation.*

Those, who believe in this newer view—myself included—would ask: "What good is it, what kind of a gift, if an individual has high ability in a certain area but doesn't apply it in different ways and settings (creativity), and improve it/develop it/use it (motivation)?" You need to *have* the ability, creatively *apply* or use the ability, and *do* something with it.

Are people truly gifted if they keep their gift inside and don't do something with it? I think not!

Now for an interesting question: What's the most important ingredient in the formula? Is it potential, creativity, or motivation? Let's take gymnastics as an example. Which of the following children is probably going to go furthest in gymnastics?

> *Child 1: incredible potential*
> *above average creativity*
> *above average motivation*
>
> ●
>
> *Child 2: above average potential*
> *incredible creativity*
> *above average motivation*

> Child 3: *above average potential*
>   *above average creativity*
>   *incredible motivation*

Now think about it. Close your eyes and think. Don't read on until you have chosen either Child 1, 2, or 3 as the most likely to go furthest in gymnastics. Were this gymnast my child I'd go for Child 3, with incredible motivation. In my mind, and the minds of most who adhere to this new view, the kids who most often go further, who are viewed by society as gifted, are the ones who are really motivated and put in the effort. Yes, the innate potential is important, as is creativity, but if children don't use what they have, if they don't practice and study and push themselves to excellence, they aren't going to take fullest advantage of their gift, and then, is it really a gift?

I know what you're thinking. You're thinking that individuals like Michael Jordan (basketball star), Madonna (singer/actress), Stephen King (author), and Madeleine Albright (U.S. Secretary of State) have so much innate potential and creativity that they really didn't have to work that hard to make it to the top in their fields. (Prior to writing this paragraph I approached my nine-year-old daughter and asked her to tell me the names of some famous women who have accomplished extraordinary things in their lives. She came up with three names: (1) President Abraham Lincoln's wife, (2) President Bill Clinton's wife, and (3) Helen Keller. I'm not terribly surprised, but a bit saddened and disappointed in myself. I need to reread and seriously consider my own recommendations for encouraging potential in females!) Well, think again. Individuals who achieve great levels of performance rarely if ever do it without outstanding work ethics (motivation and task commitment). Each of these individuals has worked incredibly hard and dedicated a major portion of their life to advancement in their profession. Success was not handed to them; it didn't fall in their laps!

So, there you have it. The children I want to discuss in this section are the ones who have significant amounts of potential, either in math, language, science, art, interpersonal skills, or any other area that might lead them to a career or hobby. They also have the ability to apply some creativity or variety in the use of those skills. And, they have and/or can be encouraged to develop the motivation to focus on improving themselves in those areas and share what they know or can do, with others.

Challenges to Maximizing Potential

Okay, your children have solid innate ability and creativity in a certain area; now the issue or question is how to turn that ability into achievement, to move from I-could-have-been-champ to I-am-the-champ, from I-could-have-really-done-something-with-my-abilities-in _____ to I'm-proud-of-what-I've-done-with-my-abilities-in _____ .

If you're lucky, your children will be raised in an environment where everything will fall into place for them, and their areas of exceptional ability will flourish into high levels of achievement. They will be internally motivated to study and practice and grow and develop in many areas. They will minimize their time spent in activities that are not growth-producing. They will take advantage of opportunities to learn, ignore negative influences, disregard nay sayers and pessimists, seek out role models and mentors, and be all that they can be. If you're lucky, very lucky, you won't have to do much except observe this wonderful process in action.

Now, wake up, and let's talk about the reality that most parents face, realities that often include ingredients from the following list.

• •

too much time spent watching television and playing videogames

difficulty motivating, coercing, moving, pushing, and coaxing them to practice or study

teachers who don't challenge them

the lack of funds to pay for private lessons, classes, and tutoring

the challenge of moving them away from other children whom we regard as negative influences, and our sometimes inability to get them to spend time with children we regard as positive influences

• •

These are some of the challenges to maximizing their areas of potential.

Consider the following.

■ Would Bach had been the child prodigy and musical master that he was if Nintendo had been around in the eighteenth century and if he had fallen in love with it and played it three hours each day?

■ Would British Prime Minister Margaret Thatcher ever have come to the position of leading her country if she had become involved with a gang in the third grade and spent the next few years hanging around with a group of girls who were angry at their parents and the world and not involved with academic learning or making a positive contribution to society?

■ Would Tiger Woods have become one of the best golfers in the world if he had never wanted to practice and his parents had dragged him onto the course and bribed him to play?

■ Would Maya Angelou have become a world-renowned poet, author, and speaker if her teachers in preschool and elementary school had not allowed her to experiment with language and encouraged her uniqueness?

The answer to each question is, probably not! Some kids are incredibly resilient; they have the ability to land on their feet, to set themselves right, almost regardless of negative influences in their lives, but parents can't count on their children being able to do this. There are real and significant challenges out there that may limit the realizing of a potentially gifted child's abilities, and we parents must be prepared to identify these challenges or obstacles and help our children overcome them.

RECOMMENDATIONS

1. Limit your children's exposure to television, especially to shows that you do not approve of.

2. If, on a regular basis, your children seem to be spending an inordinate amount of their time involved in an activity or activities that seem to be of questionable value (such as watching TV, playing Nintendo, daydreaming), attempt to find a way to limit these activities and/or work on positively redirecting them (see Chapter 4). Seek professional help if need be.

3. Make every effort to encourage your children in areas in which you perceive them to have solid potential. Provide them with interesting and appropriate activities and materials that will motivate them. When they are actively involved in study or practice, observe the conditions that exist around them (time of day, room, mood, other children they're with, materials being used, how they got started in the activity, what happened right before they became involved). Try to replicate these conditions and determine the critical motivating factors.

4. Make an effort to expose your children to caregivers and teachers who share your view of your children's potentials and who value the development of those areas. Look for caregivers and teachers who provide environments in which these potentials can flourish. Acknowledge, encourage, praise, and support these people in their efforts to maximize your children's potential.

5. Expose your children to various experiences and role models in their areas of potential. It's great if you can afford special classes or tutors, but if you can't, there are other ways. County fairs, audiotapes and CDs, museums, community events and classes, art galleries, high school sporting events…the experiences and role models are there, waiting to be discovered.

6. Make it easier for your children to be around other children who exemplify the traits you want yours to develop. Make it more difficult for them to have the opportunity or time to be around children who are negative influences on them. Take an active role in designing the world they are exposed to.

7. Look at yourself. If you aren't already learning and growing in an area or areas of your own potential, then get started. Your attitude and actions toward yourself and your own life can have an incredible influence on your children.

LEARNING DISABLED (LD)

Who Is Included in this Group?

A number of closely related learning challenges are included in the group known as *learning disabled.* Children (and adults—the condition is one that remains for life) who have learning disabilities may differ in the severity of their challenges, in the areas of learning that are affected, and/or in the ways in which they learn more and less efficiently. However, all learning disabilities share the following characteristics.

- Members of this group have at least average or above average intelligence (IQ).
- The learning challenges must be linked to brain function-ing (most commonly, deficiencies or differences in the brain's visual and/or auditory perceptions and/or memory capabilities), and are not caused primarily by linguistic or cultural differences, poor education, or another disability.
- A significant discrepancy exists between an individual's potential/intelligence and one or more of the following areas of performance.

• •

reading (including comprehension)

writing (composing thoughts into words, sentences, communications—not handwriting)

logical/mathematical reasoning or calculation.

• •

While estimates of the size of this group vary greatly, approximately 5 percent of children in U.S. schools receive spe-cial education services for this condition. While children with learning disabilities most often do learn to read, write, and per-form mathematical functions at some level, in the vast majority of cases it is a lifelong challenge and disability.

Because learning disabilities are very commonly repeated within family trees, and occur three to five times more often in males than females, the primary cause is thought to be genetic; however, researchers have not yet identified specific genes that may be involved. Other causes and combinations of causes can create learning disabilities. These include

• •

anoxia (loss of oxygen to parts of the brain) during gestation or early childhood.

brain injury and infections.

prolonged high fevers.

biochemical differences.

lead poisoning.

fetal alcohol syndrome.

• •

While it is assumed that the vast majority of individuals who have learning disabilities were born with them, the condition is rarely diagnosed prior to first or second grade, primarily because the diagnosis requires a discrepancy between ability and performance in reading, writing, and/or mathematics, areas that are rarely tested before a child is six years old. Early signs that a child may have a learning disability are

• •

delays in speech or language development.

following directions significantly less well than other children of the same age.

having memory abilities (names, songs, counting, letters) that are significantly less developed than other children of the same age.

a very jagged or uneven developmental profile (significant highs and low in areas such as verbal abilities, mathematical understanding, physical coordination, memory, and attention).

• •

Basically, what you have in learning disabilities are individuals with normal or above normal intelligence who have brains that function quite well in most ways, but with portions of their brains that don't work as well or as efficiently in some ways. The affected areas of the brain are those that relate to the development of reading and/or writing and/or mathematics.

In order for individuals with learning disabilities to perform better in those subject areas, it is necessary that they either learn to bypass the affected brain area(s) and use other brain areas for learning, and/or in some way learn to more efficiently use the brain area(s) that is affected.

Challenges to Maximizing Potential

Having a learning disability does not mean that children are destined to have lives of frustration and failure; it means that they will be more challenged than other children in the lifelong pursuit of the maximization of their potentials. Numerous successful, contributing, well-adjusted, wealthy, and famous individuals have learning disabilities. In each case they had to work harder, study longer, and survive under the burden of more frustrations and setbacks than they might have had they not had their learning disability. The challenges that will be outlined in the following paragraphs are by no means insurmountable; they just make learning, life, achievement, and the maximization of potential more challenging.

Two of many challenges for individuals with learning disabilities are (1) the extra time it takes to learn new information and perform tasks, and (2) dealing with the frustrations inherent in being different, being perceived by others as different, and in dealing with the roadblocks, challenges, and often failures that the disability creates.

All individuals with learning disabilities have a certain area or areas of their brain—areas that are involved with reading and/or writing and/or mathematics—that don't work very efficiently. Working with and around these affected brain areas takes more time and energy and what happens when you spend more time and energy on something? You have less time and perhaps less energy for other pursuits. For example, five-year-old Jodie is able to learn the names of all her cousins very easily. Her seven-year-old brother Tommy, on the other hand, has great difficulty with auditory memory. (The part of his brain that is supposed to hear and remember doesn't function nearly as efficiently as other parts of his brain.) When Mom and Dad talk about cousins, experiences with cousins, or going to see cousins, what to buy for cousins' birthday presents, Jodie is right in the conversation and can quickly picture who is being discussed. Tommy, on the other hand, needs constant reminding about who's who, and to keep him involved in the conversation and decisions, a lot of extra time needs to be invested in refreshing and working on his memory. And, as you might guess, Tommy's auditory memory difficulties also create many challenges in school and learning.

Some children (and adults) with learning disabilities have very inefficient visual systems. Letters, numbers, symbols, and pictures sometimes appear upside down and/or backwards to them. In this type of learning disability, individuals must spend much more time and energy, and move much more slowly to decipher visual messages. Even after spending more time, they still may not be certain that they are seeing something the way others see it. They may look at the word *bad* and see *dab,* or look at the symbol -> and see <-, or read the number *25* and say *52.*

Some individuals with learning disabilities have perfect visual systems but have difficulty with their auditory systems. As an example, eight-year-olds with brains that function very poorly in auditory discrimination (hearing the differences between sounds) are very challenged in learning to read and spell new words. They are forced to spend more time practicing their spelling and reading in order to succeed. Where does this time and energy come from? Well, obviously it comes from somewhere. Somewhere, somehow, for them to learn these new words they'll need to spend more time and energy.

Will the time and energy be taken away from children's pursuit of abilities and interests in sports or music? Will parents and teachers take away their play time or art time so they can work on spelling and reading? Learning inefficiencies that lie at the heart of learning disabilities require that these individuals invest much more time to learn than their level of intelligence would dictate. Extra time spent on learning basic academic skills usually takes time away from pursuing other areas of potential.

The other main issue or challenge in learning disabilities is frustration, the frustration of seeing others learn things more quickly, the frustration of making errors and having occasional misunderstandings no matter how hard you try, the frustration of being seen by others as a person who is different, as a person with a disability, rather than a person who is more normal than different—as a person with many abilities.

Individuals with learning disabilities need to understand their disabilities, and also their abilities. They need more help in learning how they learn less and more efficiently. They need to learn strategies to monitor themselves, the work they produce, their understanding, and their feelings and emotions.

RECOMMENDATIONS

1. Make every effort to discover and help your children discover the ways in which they learn more efficiently.

2. Share these learning strengths with your children's care providers and teachers.

3. At as young an age as possible endeavor to find the areas of your children's brains that are most challenged and discover ways to build up/reinforce those areas, in low-pressure, engaging, fun, high success ways, so that they will be better prepared to handle the learning challenges that must be faced.

4. Do not focus on your children's disabilities at the expense of their abilities. Yes, the areas of disability will require more time and energy and attention, but it is also important to focus on developing their abilities and areas of potential, from which their careers and leisure pursuits will more than likely emerge!

5. Monitor and caution caregivers and teachers when, in their desire to help build success in your children's areas of disability, they minimize attention to and instruction in your children's areas of ability.

6. Learning disabilities last forever. Consult resources and find ways to teach your children about themselves so that they can assume responsibility for their own learning and growth.

ATTENTION-DEFICIT/HYPERACTIVITY DISORDERS (ADHD)

Who Is Included in this Group?

ADHD, sometimes called ADD with or without hyperactivity, is a condition that may exist when a child (or adult) has far more difficulty than other children of the same age, over an extended period of time, in at least six of the nine traits on either or both of the following lists.

- *Symptoms of inattention:*

    1. poor attention to detail, makes careless mistakes
    2. difficulty sustaining attention or focusing
    3. poor listening
    4. poor following through on instructions; inability to finish tasks
    5. difficulty organizing
    6. avoiding or disliking tasks that require sustained attention
    7. frequently losing belongings
    8. becoming easily distracted
    9. forgetfulness

- *Symptoms of hyperactivity and impulsivity:*

    1. often fidgeting with hands or feet or squirming
    2. often leaving one's seat
    3. frequent and inappropriate running around and climbing
    4. difficulty playing quietly
    5. being often on the go/driven by motor
    6. talking excessively
    7. often blurting out answers
    8. difficulty awaiting turn
    9. often interrupting or intruding

While the diagnosis may be made at any age, even into adulthood, the symptoms are supposedly present before the age of seven years old. Most children (and adults) who have ADHD have what is referred to as the combined type (at least six of nine symptoms from both lists—inattentive and hyperactive/ impulsive). This combined type is sometimes referred to as ADD with hyperactivity. However, some children (and adults) have ADHD-predominantly inattentive (sometimes referred to as ADD or ADD without hyperactivity) while others have ADHD-predominantly hyperactive (often referred to as simply hyperactive).

Estimates of the prevalence of ADHD (all types) vary widely, but most in the field believe that 3 to 5 percent of all children have the condition. Prevalence of the condition in adulthood is a bit lower than the 3 to 5 percent figure because, for reasons that are not yet perfectly clear, some teenagers seem to grow out of ADHD and others adapt to it so well that the label no longer seems to fit. However, for significantly over 50 percent of children who exhibit the symptoms of ADHD as children, a lifetime condition exists.

The causes of ADHD seem to be varied, with genetic/ familial factors very probably being the most common. Research has not yet found the specific gene or genes involved, but the condition is common in some family trees and rare in others, which has led researchers to a search for inheritable factors. Other possible causes are

• •

anoxia (loss of oxygen to parts of the brain) during gestation or early childhood.

brain injury or infections.

prolonged high fevers.

biochemical differences.

lead poisoning.

fetal alcohol syndrome.

• •

Yes, you're right, this is the same list you found under possible causes of learning disabilities. The reason is not that the author's computer stutters or that the author is lazy. The lists are the same because both LD and ADHD are results of variations in brain functioning, and this list includes a variety of conditions that can assault the brain and its functioning. At the present time it is unproven, yet assumed, that learning disabilities are more related to the structure and pathways within parts of the brain, while ADHD is more related to the chemicals that coat those structures and pathways or to a difference in blood flow through certain parts of the brain. However, these are yet to be proven theories that are presently being investigated.

It should also be pointed out that there is an overlap between the two conditions—LD and ADHD. It appears that in the neighborhood of 20 to 25 percent of children who have one have both.

LEARNING DISABILITIES
ATTENTION DEFICIT/HYPERACTIVE DISORDERS

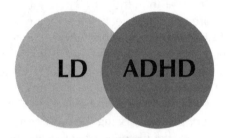

At the present time, males are diagnosed with ADHD approximately three times more often than females.

Challenges to Maximizing Potential

Most ADHD is set into motion/or finds its origin at conception. Or one might say that the seed is planted very early. In all cases the symptoms must have existed prior to the age of seven. Now, let's imagine a child who demonstrates many or most of the symptoms listed previously and exhibits them far more often and intensely than other children of the same age. My guess is (and my guess is based on working with many, many children who have ADHD and also speaking with dozens of parents of children who have the condition) that during the early childhood years most of these children will experience far more of the following than their peers who live without ADHD.

• •

fighting with and rejection from peers
parental disapproval and anger

day-care, preschool, and elementary school discipline, suspension, and expulsion

negative comments and severe discipline

difficulty finding and retaining competent babysitters

attacks on self-image

personal injury

academic and general school deficits and failure

retention in kindergarten or first grade (to give them time to grow out of it, which they usually don't)

misunderstandings

disappointments and failures due to not understanding or following directions or acting too quickly

parental stress (see above for possible causes)

• •

These kids are really challenged. If the ADHD is not dealt with early and effectively, their chances of maximizing potential, in any area, are severely diminished.

RECOMMENDATIONS

1. If you think your child may have ADHD consult your pediatrician and get referrals to see a specialist (a child psychiatrist or psychologist). There are no drugs or medical treatments that can make the ADHD go away, but certain drugs may temporarily ease some of the condition's symptoms and set a stage where more positive relationships can be formed and learning can take place more easily and efficiently.

2. Look for more structured, orderly, organized, and consistent day-care centers, preschools, and elementary classrooms, educational environments that will help them keep themselves under control.

3. Consider organizing your home (including your children's rooms), daily schedules, and play and study environments in ways that will better accommodate their attention and activity level challenges and needs.

4. Help them discover areas of ability that they possess. Remember, there are two sides to every coin. Hyperactivity is a disadvantage in some situations, for certain tasks, but a real advantage for others—how can they use their hyperactivity? A short attention span and a tendency to shift attention from here, to there, and here, to there is a disadvantage in some environments, for certain ways of behaving and learning, but can also be used to one's advantage in positive ways. Help them find these ways.

5. There are many great role models and highly successful people who have various types and levels of ADHD. Become aware of them and see to it that your children become aware of them. Learn how they have used their ADHD to their advantage.

6. Protect your children, when possible, from situations in which they are more likely to experience failure. Find ways to strengthen them (counseling, success-oriented experiences, focusing on abilities) to better deal with the failures and frustrations they will face in their futures.

MENTALLY RETARDED (MR)/ DEVELOPMENTALLY DISABLED (DD)

Who Is Included in this Group?

Mental retardation, sometimes called developmental disability, includes individuals who learn very slowly (in about the lowest 2 percent on IQ tests) and have significant difficulty (again, the lowest 2 percent or so), compared to others of their age, with basic life skills (*adaptive behavior*), such as dressing, eating, and communicating.

The severity of the condition ranges from mild, to moderate, to severe and profound. Those who are mildly retarded usually have the capability to live independently or semi-independently, hold down a job, make friends, engage in social interactions and hobbies, and lead full, rich, and rewarding lives. Those with moderate and severe retardation are more challenged in these areas, and the profoundly retarded require constant care and supervision throughout life for the most basic of needs (feeding, toileting, bathing).

There are many possible causes of retardation, including

• •

environmental influences.
infections.
brain disease.
chromosomal abnormalities.
psychiatric disorders.
gestational disorders.
metabolism or nutrition.

• •

The condition is irreversible—it never goes away—however, as with most children and adults, a rich and stimulating environment can help them in realizing more of their innate potential.

Challenges to Maximizing Potential

The primary challenge here is patience. The one factor that all individuals with mental retardation have in common is that they learn slowly. Some learn slowly, and others learn very, very, very slowly. The question is, how much time and effort can and will parents, care providers, and teachers put into the education and training of these children?

Assuming that a child with mental retardation was interested and motivated to play the trumpet, or study a second language, or play tennis, or learn geometry, that child would have to be very patient and receive instruction from individuals who were very patient.

This brings up the factor of time, once again. How much time is a person willing to spend on learning and developing a new skill, and where will that time come from?

Parents and professionals involved with mental retardation most often place basic life skills at the top of the priority list. The usual thought is to spend more time teaching and training these children to do things that, if they didn't learn to do them on their own, would have to be done to and for them by others.

Once it appears that basic personal care skills will be sufficiently mastered, the next level of concern and attention is usually employability skills. With all this time and attention going into the basics, it's no wonder that areas of hidden potential, areas such as art, music, appreciation of nature, and dance, often receive less attention.

RECOMMENDATIONS

1. Remember, every word in this book applies to your children too. Children with mental retardation are more like other children their own age than they are like adults who are retarded.

2. Make every effort to focus on at least one area of hidden potential your children have. Start looking for this area when they are very young.

3. As you and special educators write your children's individual family service plans (IFSPs) and individual education plans (IEPs) include at least one goal, each year, in an area of hidden potential. Don't allow 100 percent of the focus to be on their disabilities.

4. Search out role models with similar levels of retardation who can serve as mentors to your children and reminders to you of the possibilities.

5. Remember that learning and growth in mental retardation is more like a marathon than a 100-yard dash. You need to keep your focus and attention on where you are; don't push yourself or your children too hard. Don't burn out; slow down and take breaks when needed. Constantly remind yourself that no matter how slow the progress, no matter how distant your goals seem to be, you need to keep moving forward, like the "Little Engine that Could," just keep on chuggin'!

6. Celebrate the little victories and joys, no matter how small they may seem and how far you may still be from your goals. We need to reward ourselves along the way.

EMOTIONALLY/BEHAVIORALLY DISORDERED

Who Is Included in this Group?

This group requires little introduction. Parents of these children know who they are and the challenges they face. Whether or not your child actually qualifies for one of the many subcategories or labels in this group, you're going to need professional help for the children who are affected, yourself, your other children, and your marriage or relationships with significant others. If you are concerned that your children may be emotionally/behaviorally disordered, you should consult your pediatrician and meet with a licensed child psychiatrist or psychologist.

Challenges to Maximizing Potential

Children in this group may be very quiet, shy, and withdrawn or loud, unruly, outgoing, and dangerous to themselves and others. They may seem overly concerned with what others think of them and hypersensitive to the glances, looks, and attitudes of others, or emotionally detached, distant, and insensitive to the world around them. They may be victims or predators. Regardless of which of these descriptions match certain children, they all face similar challenges.

The primary challenges to encouraging potential in children with emotional/behavioral disorders are (1) getting them involved in positive, growth-producing activities, (2) enticing them to dedicate themselves to advancement in their areas of potential, and (3) finding someone with the skill and patience to work with them; this includes all types of care providers and professionals.

Some of the children in this group have low self concepts; others are very detached from their own feelings and personal needs; still others are so involved with fantasies and their present emotional states that they have difficulty concentrating on study and the practice required to develop new skills, difficulty becoming involved. Moving them away from these negative and nonproductive thoughts and feelings can be a real challenge. Other children in this group have so much anger and hostility that it's difficult for them to calm down, center in, and really work at developing an area of themselves.

Finding the right people who can help care for and teach these children is perhaps even a greater challenge. Children with emotional/behavioral disorders are often very frustrating to work with. Encouraging them to get involved and then to stay involved with positive efforts takes skill, sensitivity, individual attention, flexibility, and patience. Both in group settings with other children and when working one-on-one, it's often very hard to get these children to focus and get down to work; to break out of their own limited mental worlds and become productively involved.

RECOMMENDATIONS

1. Parents, care providers, and teachers of these children need first and foremost to stay in good mental, emotional, and physical shape themselves. No matter how much you care, or how skilled you are, the ups and downs are usually frequent and dramatic. It takes a strong, healthy, together person to work with these children over the long haul!

2. It has been said that *genius* is the twin brother/sister of *insanity*. Do your children's areas of insanity relate to any realms that might be considered genius? Are there any professions or hobbies that are better suited to your children's areas of genius/insanity?

3. The chances of success in involving them with areas of greater potential are heightened if they are led in the direction of interests that are compatible with who they are. If a loud, active, acting-out child is interested in playing both the drums and the guitar, the chances are better that the child will get and stay involved with the drums, rather than the guitar. (Sorry parents, but it's true!)

4. While these children require huge amounts of sensitivity on the part of those who work with them, they usually also need more structure, order, clearer limits and guidelines, and more reinforcement than other children. Behavioral contracting, reward/reinforcement programs, and consistency are usually recommended approaches to moving them into involvement in more positive, productive endeavors.

5. Seek the professional advice of a child psychologist, social worker, or counselor to help you structure programs and routines such as those described in the previous recommendation.

PHYSICAL AND/OR SENSORY CHALLENGES

Who Is Included in this Group?

While a very diverse group, each with its own challenges to realizing potential, this section will briefly discuss the following:

- the blind—children whose visual systems are severely impaired
- the deaf—children whose hearing is severely impaired
- the physically challenged—children whose ambulation /movement through space and/or ability to control their body movements are impaired. This group includes children with cerebral palsy, muscular dystrophy, loss of limb, and so on.
- the health impaired—children who have limited strength, energy, or alertness due to their health, or are dependent on medications or medical technology to support their lives. This group includes children with heart conditions, various cancers, HIV and AIDS, tuberculosis, asthma, sickle-cell anemia, epilepsy, diabetes, muscular dystrophy.

Challenges to Maximizing Potential

The primary reason these various and diverse groups fit together within this section is that one of the most critical challenges to their maximization of potential is exposure. They often face challenges in being exposed to the stimuli and environments that will help them learn and grow. Without special attention and extra effort, children in each of these groups may miss certain experiences that might be beneficial to both their all-around growth and development as well as the maximization of particular areas of potential.

Exposure. What do I mean by *exposure?* Let's look at some examples.

Susan is two years old and blind. Without extra encouragement and an extra effort to bring a variety of experiences to her, it is likely that she will not move around—not experiment with walking, jumping, running, tumbling, rolling, kicking, throwing, and catching—as much as other two-year-olds. It is likely that many of the words she uses—words like elephant, glistening, locomotive, rainbow, and furnace—will be limited in the images they bring to her mind, their use, and meaning. It is likely that her experience of the world, the way she sees it in her mind, will have many holes and many distortions. However, a concerted effort to expose her to experiences in which her lack of vision may limit her will certainly fill many of those holes and add a sense of clarity and understanding to many of those distortions.

Tommy is four years old and deaf. He will also face the challenge of exposure. Depending on the severity of his deafness, he will very probably need to learn some form of sign language in order to communicate with other people, or risk not being exposed to many of the joys of communicating with other human beings and benefiting from their insights, knowledge, understanding, and guidance. He may need to learn to read lips in order to understand the conversations of people who don't use sign language, or run the risk of not benefiting from exposure to their verbal exchanges and his relationships with them. Without being able to hear oncoming cars, horns, bicycles, and footsteps, he will have to learn how to pay special attention to other sensory signs, or be limited in his movements outside of his home and risk limited exposure to and safety in other environments. Tommy's challenges are different from Susan's challenges to exposure, but similar in that extra attention must be paid to his education and training in order to expose him to a full and balanced life.

Wendy is seven years old and has severe, quadriplegic, spastic cerebral palsy. It took her three years to learn to roll over and now, at the age of seven, one of her major life goals is to be able to feed herself with a spoon. Had her parents, care providers, and teachers not, over the past seven years, frequently moved her body position and gone out of their way to place objects of interest and educational value within her view and grasp, she would not be the curious, worldly, computer-literate, Internet surfing, gifted, and academically superb young lady she is today. As a matter of fact, had the adult world around her not gone out of its way to expose Wendy to experiences and knowledge, had they just let her fend for herself, her cerebral palsy might well have led her to a life of mental retardation, a life very different from the gifted status that most who know her believe she has claim to. Exposure. Wendy couldn't get it on her own, but her parents and other wonderful people made sure she had it!

• •

Peter was born with hemophilia (a hereditary tendency to bruising and difficulty controlling bleeding). Due to a blood transfusion in his second year of life, he became HIV positive and soon after developed AIDS. He bruises and bleeds often and easily, has a fluctuating and usually weak immune system, and rarely goes for more than a few weeks without being confined to bed for several days. He has been in and out of hospitals his entire life. Because he is very susceptible to injury and infection, his attendance in preschool and now in elementary school has been an on-again, off-again thing. For the past three years he has been home or in the hospital far more often than in school. Yet, his parents have seen to it that he has been exposed to a huge chunk of life. During periods of greater health and energy, and with people who did not appear to be ill, he has been exposed to, played with, and formed caring relationships with many children and adults. Again, within the limits of his health and immune system's ups and downs, he has traveled, played some sports and games of all kinds, visited libraries and museums, and shared numerous joys with his family and loved ones. He has and is leading as full and normal a life as possible. The fullness and normalcy of his life, however, has required his parents to pay constant and intense attention to different ways Peter could be exposed to people and experiences.

Exposure. Without special attention to providing children in these groups with exposure to specific experiences, many aspects of their growth and development, only one of which is the encouragement of their areas of particular potential, would be in jeopardy.

RECOMMENDATIONS

1. Analyze how your children's exceptional needs impact on how they experience life, and make every attempt to expose them to the various types of stimulation they are challenged in accessing.

2. Start early. Begin providing compensatory stimulation and experiences as soon as possible. The sooner you start providing them with needed experiences the better the chances that the handicapping effects of their disability will be minimized.

3. As has been the case with all of the special populations in this section, provide your children with role models who have similar conditions and yet are leading full, rich, and rewarding lives.

4. Seek professional help or, rather, seek the help of professionals/ specialists. Early stimulation programs, school district special education teachers and consultants, occupational therapists, physical therapists, recreation therapists, speech and language pathologists, physicians, support groups, and so on.

5. Follow the advice you found in the previous ten chapters. Remember, your special children are children first, and special or exceptional second!

6. Because your children do not have full use of their vision, hearing, limbs, or bodies, they will probably be quite challenged to achieve in certain areas (for example, being blind and playing baseball, being deaf and conducting an orchestra, being physically handicapped and becoming a ballerina). Therefore, it is all that much more important to find their areas of potential, or ability; search long and hard to find and help them appreciate and develop these areas.

CULTURALLY AND/OR LINGUISTICALLY DIFFERENT

Who Is Included in this Group?

Two different yet often overlapping groups will be discussed together in this, the final section of groups at risk. These two groups are

■ children who are raised in a situation where the culture shared with them within their family/home setting is dramatically different from the culture at large.

■ children who are raised in a situation where their primary caregivers do not speak the language of the land and the language spoken to the children at home is different from the predominant language spoken outside of their home.

The first group includes immigrants to a new country or culture, families who wish to retain the culture of their homeland and ancestors and not be assimilated into the culture where they now live, religious and communal groups whose ways and traditions are very different from those that exist in the surrounding, predominant culture, and the homeless.

The second group is self-explanatory. Children raised in a home where they are spoken to in a language different from the language that predominates outside their home are not necessarily, but quite often, either delayed or limited in their proficiency with the local language.

Challenges to Maximizing Potential

The primary challenges to the maximization of potential in these groups is their ability to access all that the surrounding environment has to offer. Being from a different culture and/or language background can be limiting as far as inclusion in society and full use of nearby resources. A few examples should help to clarify this challenge of access.

The newspapers advertise an arts and crafts festival to be held in the local high school's cafeteria, but child A's parents don't take their child, either because they can't read the newspaper or because they've never been in a high school and feel afraid or intimidated.

The local Arts Center has a free photographic exhibit depicting homes and lifestyles from around the world, but child B's parents come from a culture where only the wealthy and educated are allowed in centers like this, so they don't realize that it is available to them and their children.

Child C's first grade class is studying folk tales from around the world, but C's proficiency in English is very limited and he/she doesn't understand most of what's going on in the stories and discussions.

The YMCA is offering free-of-charge swimming lessons for all three-, four-, and five-year-olds. Child D's parents are concerned that Christian doctrine may be a part of the swim program, in some subtle, hidden way. They belong to a particular religious group that does not allow exposure to other doctrines, and therefore will not allow their child to take the swimming lessons.

When parents strive to retain their culture and language, they sometimes view their children's venturing into the predominant culture and language as threats. There is sometimes a fear that as their children become more involved in the predominant culture and language they will be lost from the family; they will become strangers. This fear, coupled with a tendency to not fully utilize the cultural, leisure, and educational resources of the area, may insulate and limit children.

The adult members of groups such as those described in this section are sometimes threatened by the thought of their children becoming something very different from themselves and their extended family or group members. These adults sometimes intentionally discourage their children's strivings to investigate and develop areas of their potential, if development in those areas might threaten the status quo of the larger family or group unit. There may be a significant force leading children to not be different; to not investigate their strengths and desires too much; and to not veer much from the insular group.

Many believe however, that it is possible to retain one's culture and language and still actively participate in the surrounding society. Many people from culturally and linguistically divergent backgrounds encourage their children to explore, grow, learn, and develop themselves as human beings. It is for these individuals that the following recommendations are made.

RECOMMENDATIONS

1. If you want your children to someday enter and be a part of the larger society, allow and encourage them to experience that society, to learn about it, to understand it, and to speak its language.

2. If you believe that your children may possess an area of potential that is incompatible with your values, consider ways in which their potential might be applied to some area of achievement within your value or cultural system.

3. If you approve of your children entering the society at large, to experience all it has to offer, yet you feel uncomfortable accompanying them, find someone who can and will. Perhaps an older sibling or relative, a friend, parents of one of your children's acquaintances, or a surrogate parent or Big Brother or Big Sister from a local community agency such as the YMCA, YWCA, Hispanic Chamber of Commerce, the Elks club, or the Shriners.

4. Contact or have a friend, relative, or acquaintance contact for you, a community agency such as Social Services, your local county board, or the local school district, to learn about programs that might be available to help teach your children about the local culture, enhance their language skills, or investigate areas of interest (potential).

SUMMARY

The first ten chapters of this book made numerous recommendations for encouraging potential in young children—in all young children. Ideas such as providing children with a variety of learning opportunities, using consequences rather than punishments, encouraging and encouraging, and following their lead, apply to all children. Children are first and foremost children, more like other children, like all other children, than like adults from their own particular sex, or race, or disability group.

Despite this, special attention needs to be paid to children who fall into groups that may find more challenges in maximizing their potential. The groups addressed in this chapter and the primary challenges they face are as follows.

- *Girls:* traditional expectations of appropriate roles and behavior
- *The gifted:* finding the will or motivation to excel when they can get by with less effort
- *Various groups of individuals with exceptional needs:* finding the time and energy to work on an area or areas of ability, despite the fact that so much energy and extra time also needs to be invested in minimizing the handicapping effects of disabilities, and also finding ways to move beyond disabilities and expose them to stimuli that will help these individuals learn and grow
- *Culturally and linguistically different:* access to the resources and learning that exists around them

The most important recommendation made in this chapter centers around awareness. As parents become more aware of the potentially limiting effects that membership in one of these at-risk groups may have, they will naturally begin the process of minimizing these effects and therefore heighten the chances that their children will more fully reach their potentials.

CHAPTER 12

Summing Up

While we haven't met, I believe that I know something about you. What I know is that you are a searcher, a person who is looking for ideas to help you be a better parent. You take your parenting job seriously, and have a deep desire to create a positive, growth-producing, loving, caring environment for your children. Hopefully, this book has revealed to you that I feel the same way.

We *can* make a difference! We can make a difference in who we are as well as in who our children will become, and the more complete and actualized we and our children are, the better our world will be.

It is my deepest hope that this book has interested and entertained you, teased your imagination, given you some useful ideas, and enhanced your understanding of yourself, your children, and how to encourage potential. I know that writing this book has done all of these things for me.

Before saying good-bye, bear with me for just a few more pages as I review the most critical concepts and recommendations.

Potential

In order to help our children make the most they can of their lives, we, their parents, must learn about and understand, and help our children learn about and understand, themselves. This knowledge can help us design experiences that will lead them to utilizing more of their potential, and the self-knowledge and understanding they gain may become powerful tools to help them find meaning and direction in life and make important choices. Through identifying areas of personal potential parents and children have more data to help make decisions on careers, hobbies to pursue, subjects to study, and future plans or goals.

Being aware that your children have significant potential in a particular area isn't enough. Parents need to have techniques to help bring that potential out, to help actualize it. Parents need to organize environments that keep children actively, productively, creatively, and joyously involved and aware that their efforts have value, and that value lies both in experiencing the process as well as the product of their efforts.

Encouragement

One approach to enhancing this involvement in and attitude toward experiences and learning was described under the heading of encouragement, including the specific technique referred to as **en**couragement. Encouragement is one of the most powerful tools parents can use to nurture and bring to life their children's potential.

Consequences

Along with encouragement, it is recommended that parents use consequences. Consequences, as opposed to punishment, teach children to look within themselves, rather than to others, when considering their actions and the effects those actions may have. Consequences are also far better teachers of responsibility than are punishments. In order for parents to do the most they can at the job of encouraging potential in their children, they must help them, in every way possible, to learn to look within and be responsible for their decisions, actions, and the results of what they do.

Follow Their Lead, Positive Redirection

Two other techniques, follow their lead, and positive redirection, furnish parents with approaches to provide their children with more practice and in-depth exploration and learning. By utilizing these techniques, parents will have more understanding and trust in the positive values of their children's self-directed play, be in possession of techniques that, when the occasion arises, may help them slightly change or alter the direction of that play, and, as was the goal on every page of this book, help encourage potential in their children.

Emerging Skills

If we are to truly encourage potential in children, the sooner we start the better. The earlier we identify and nurture children's strengths, as well as paying attention to and remediating areas of development that may emerge slowly, the better. It is of critical importance that, in the first few years of life, children develop solid foundations for later, more academic and formal instruction and learning.

Modeling

Another important component of encouraging potential, one that requires you to be the best you can be, the most whole, most complete, most loving, most concerned, most intelligent, most positive, most achieving, most appreciating, most focused, most evolved, most productive, and on and on, is modeling. As the adage goes, "actions speak louder than words." If the adults who are raising children are living and exemplifying that which they hope their children to become, children will watch, listen, and be encouraged to behave in similar ways. If these adults, who act as primary role models for the children they are raising, are actively and productively involved in improving themselves, then the children with whom they interact will see this and be encouraged to behave in like ways. The sum total of most of the other, various techniques described in this book may not be as powerful as modeling. If our children love, admire, and respect us, which is usually the case, the person they perceive us to be is one of the most critical variables affecting who they will be.

Building Responsibility

Among the most important qualities we model for children are striving for self-improvement, taking chances, making sound decisions, and taking responsibility for those decisions. When our children see us taking charge of our lives, working for things we want, planning, preparing, boldly facing challenges, handling little defeats, and enjoying successes, they become more aware of their own possibilities and begin forming concepts of how to move in a positive direction, how to grow, how to live their lives.

We want them to learn from who and what we are, but this doesn't happen all at once; it's a slow process that often requires our children to experience some pain, friction, and failure. We want and need to nurture and protect them, but we also need to teach them to be strong and to nurture and protect themselves. If we do too much for them, for too long, we run the risk of building an overdependence on us and creating in them the attitude that may last (to some degree) forever, that Mommy or Daddy will take care of me; they'll make things right. This attitude is one that encourages dependence and weakness, not a strong sense of responsibility and potential.

Care Providers and Teachers

Part of this nurturing process includes establishing environments for our children that are as consistently reinforcing as possible. Whenever possible we want to diminish or remove negative influences and significant hurdles from their paths. (Once again, we need to find a balance between challenge and frustration, between too easy and too hard.) As was discussed in the chapters on potential and encouragement, children enter this world with different amounts of potential in different areas, and differing degrees or types of sensitivities to the environments they encounter (differing levels of need for encouragement). Some children have such incredible potentials, and need so little outside encouragement, that they will flourish despite a poor teacher or poor teachers, while others balance near the edge, a hairbreadth away from becoming motivated and turned on to be their best, and that same hairbreadth away from giving up, and settling for an easier path, a path in which they will only take advantage of a small portion of their potential. Because it is usually impossible for parents to be sure which group their children fall into, they must do all they can to assure that their children spend as much time as possible with teachers and other role models who will provide enriching and supportive environments, people who will highlight the possibilities, rather than constantly remind children of roadblocks and limitations.

Teaching/Tutoring Techniques

You're the key player in your children's education, but, you usually won't be and don't have to be the dispenser of all knowledge, the fountain of all information, or the finest teacher on earth. Ideally you will work well in the role as a teacher/tutor to your children, but your teaching and tutoring techniques are not the most critical variables in encouraging their potential. You can actually be a rather mediocre or poor teacher/tutor yourself, and still do a good job of encouraging potential. The good news is that identifying areas of potential, encouraging, using consequences rather than punishment, following their lead, supporting the emerging skills philosophy, modeling, fostering a strong sense of responsibility, and selecting your children's teachers, in the vast majority of cases, are more important than your own ability to serve as the teacher, or tutor, or guide.

Your job is to provide as rich, stable, and positively challenging an environment as possible, but you don't need to be the one to coax or push all the knowledge and skills into their heads.

While being the teacher/tutor will probably not be your primary job, there will be many opportunities for you to serve in this capacity. When those opportunities arise I recommend that you use the techniques described in Chapter 9.

Consistency

The topic of consistency is of greater importance in the encouragement of potential than in other areas of learning because such a significant part of the maximization of potential is dependent on psychological and social factors. Most children do at least all right in their area(s) of potential; however, many of them slide along on their innate ability and never come near to tapping the aptitude they actually possess. If we, the significant adults in children's lives, really wish to assist them in optimizing their ability, we need to pay particular attention to how they interact in a variety of settings. We need to try to enhance their learning and motivation in as many ways as possible, consistency being one of those ways.

Groups at Risk

Knowledge is power. The more we know about ourselves, our children, teaching, learning, our environment, and our society, the more knowledge we have and the better able we will be to deal with situations as they arise—to make decisions. Many in our society treat females differently than males; schools and the work world are very often more hospitable to good readers and writers than to those with deficits in these areas; people who are blind or deaf or otherwise physically disabled are challenged in ways very different from those who are emotionally disordered. To be aware of these differences can help parents more effectively structure their children's lives. Taking a focused look at the at-risk groups into which your children may fall should help you bring into greater clarity the specific environmental factors that you must be aware of to maximize their areas of potential.

FINAL RECOMMENDATIONS

1. Provide your children with a varied, rich, and stimulating environment, beginning at birth or before.

2. Remember that success leads to success and failure leads to failure. Set your children up for success.

3. Make an effort to teach your children to problem solve, evaluate their own performance, and serve as their own supporters and critics. Guiding, coaxing, helping, and rescuing children are all acceptable approaches, but approaches that need to be used with caution. Beware of making a habit of doing too much for them and/or helping them out of situations their own behavior has created. When you do step in, be aware that in solving the short-term problem you may not be helping in the long-term solution.

4. Beware of being too pushy, of rushing children into experiences they aren't ready for. Be patient.

5. Be the best, most complete person you can be; your children look at you as a model of what an adult is.

6. Take a deep breath and think before you help your children, ask a question, respond to behavior, or make a request.

7. Talk to key people who interact with you and your children and express to them your desire to reinforce, and have them reinforce your children's areas of potential. Try to enlist their support.

EXPANDED GLOSSARY

attention-deficit/hyperactivity disorders (ADHD) sometimes called ADD with or without hyperactivity, a condition that may exist when a child (or adult) has far more difficulty than other children of the same age, over an extended period of time, in at least six of the nine traits in either or both of the following areas:

Symptoms of inattention: (1) has poor attention to detail—makes careless mistakes, (2) has difficulty sustaining attention, (3) does not listen well, (4) does not follow through on instructions and often does not finish tasks, (5) has difficulty in organizing, (6) avoids or dislikes tasks that require sustained attention, (7) loses things, (8) is easily distracted, or (9) is forgetful.

Symptoms of hyperactivity and impulsivity: (1) often fidgets with hands or feet or squirms, (2) often leaves seat, (3) frequently and inappropriately runs about and climbs about, (4) has difficulty playing quietly, (5) is often on the go or seems driven by motor, (6) talks excessively, (7) often blurts out answers, (8) has difficulty awaiting turn, or (9) often interrupts or intrudes.

consequence something produced by or the result of a cause, or that necessarily follows from specified conditions.

Applied consequences may appear from the outside to be exactly the same as logical consequences, however they're different. In applied consequences the children are not brought into the process of deciding on the consequence(s). You tell them what the consequence will be, and, if you have any doubt that they will understand the logic in your consequence, briefly explain how and why it fits with what they have done.

Consequences and punishment are both responses to undesired actions or misbehavior in order to diminish the frequency or intensity of those actions or misbehavior. The primary difference between the two is that consequences are related in some way to the action or misbehavior, while punishments usually are not.

Logical consequences require that both you and your children invest some mental energy and time discussing and deciding on what the consequence(s) will be for a certain behavior, or certain behaviors.

Natural consequences occur naturally, without any intervention from you. Your children learn their lesson immediately, from nature, or another child, or other sources.

delayed gratification patience to work on goals that take time to accomplish.

diurnal rhythms certain times of the day when individuals are more capable or less capable of performing certain tasks, when their energy and awareness levels tend to rise and fall, and when they are inclined to experience different moods, attitudes, or feelings.

emerging skills philosophy that believes that all, or most skills or abilities begin their development at birth (if not before) and then mature and are refined throughout childhood and adult life.

enabling action of people or forces outside of an individual that set up an environment that makes it easier for that individual to be a certain way, or continue certain behavior, either positive or negative.

encouragement a combination of attitudes and techniques one can use to identify, support, and motivate your children's performance and development in many different areas. Encouragement includes techniques such as giving positive reinforcement (smiles, praise, rewards), establishing interesting and motivating environments, making sure that children experience success, providing positive models that they may wish to emulate, allowing for opportunities to use knowledge and skills in useful ways in the real world, providing **en**couragement, and a vast array of other strategies.

encouragement when **en** is in bold type, a subset of encouragement. It is a specific technique, the goal of which is to coax children to look within themselves and find personal gratification in their efforts and accomplishments. **En**couragement is like reinforcement and rewards, in that its goal is to support or urge or motivate positive behaviors; it is different, however, in that reinforcement and rewards come from the outside, most often from parents and teachers, while the goal in **en**couragement is to set the children up as their own reinforcers or rewarders, to get them to feel good, from within, about what they are doing.

environment sometimes referred to as upbringing or nurture, includes many different factors. Among the most important of these are the following, which frequently overlap one another: nutrition and health; sensory stimulation (including the senses of taste, smell, touch, movement/balance, hearing, and seeing), mental stimulation (including language and thought); relationships with parents, siblings, relatives, and others; and cultural experiences, awareness, and sensitivity.

following their lead making an effort whenever possible to allow children to determine the type of play or work they will become involved in and the direction that play or work will take, and then joining in on the activity they have created.

learning disabilities a number of closely related learning challenges that share the following characteristics: members of this group have at least average or above average intelligence (IQ); the learning challenges must be linked to brain functioning; a significant discrepancy must exist between an individual's potential/intelligence and performance in reading (including comprehension), writing (composing thoughts into words, sentences, communications) and/or logical/mathematical reasoning or calculation.

locus of control children's perceptions of how their actions affect outcomes: Are they in control or is their life and the things that happen to them ruled by outside forces, such as parents, teachers, other children, God, luck?

mental retardation sometimes called developmental disabilities; includes individuals who learn very slowly (in the lowest 2 percent or so on IQ tests) and have significant difficulties, compared to others of their age, with basic life skills (called adaptive behaviors), such as dressing, eating, and communicating.

modeling tendency of children to observe significant people in their lives (most notably parents) and adopt attitudes and behaviors similar to those individuals.

positive redirection carefully and subtly adding to or slightly changing the direction of children's play or work; for example, when the activity they are involved in seems to have begun deteriorating or moving in a negative direction, or when the parent/teacher feels a compelling need to change the topic or get in more skill or academic practice.

potential ceiling limit, extreme, very best one could ever possibly be in a given skill, ability, trait, or characteristic.

questions

> **Closed/close end questions** yield short, to-the-point answers.
>
> **Open/open end questions** allow children to think more and come up with more original and often longer answers. *Higher level questions* are usually open end and require children to demonstrate that they understand something, rather than simply have memorized it, and are able to use and apply their understanding to other situations, analyze information, compare and contract, relate new learning to old learning; and evaluate problems. They make children think.

reaction formation decision of children to be or do the exact opposite that they see us being or doing.

resilience personal strength or capacity to succeed against the odds; to achieve despite roadblocks, barriers, and challenges.

values those qualities, things, thoughts, and beliefs that a person or culture hold in regard, or deem to be important.

BIBLIOGRAPHY

Adler, Bill Jr. *Tell Me a Fairy Tale: A Parent's Guide to Telling Magical and Mythical Stories.* New York: Penguin Books, 1995.

Amabile, Teresa A. *Growing Up Creative: Nurturing a Lifetime of Creativity.* Buffalo, New York: Creative Education Foundation, 1989.

Armstrong, Thomas. *In Their Own Way: Discovering and Encouraging Your Child's Own Personal Learning Style.* New York: G.P. Putnam, 1987.

Baldwin, Bruce. *Beyond the Cornucopia Kids: How to Raise Healthy, Achieving Children.* Wilmington, NC: Direction Dynamics, 1988.

Barkley, Russell A. *Attention-Deficit Hyperactivity Disorder: a Handbook for Diagnosis and Treatment.* New York: The Guilford Press, 1990.

——————————. *Taking Charge of ADHD: The Complete, Authoritative Guide for Parents.* New York: The Guilford Press, 1995.

Beck, Joan. *How to Raise a Brighter Child: The Case for Early Learning.* New York: Pocket Books, 1967.

Belsky, Jay, R. Lerner, and G. Spanier. *The Child in the Family.* Menlo Park, CA: Addison Wesley, 1984.

Berends, Polly Berrien. *Gently Lead: How to Teach Your Children About God While Finding Out Yourself.* New York: Harper Perennial, 1991.

Berne, Patricia, and L. Savary. *Building Self-Esteem in Children.* New York: Crossroad Publishing Company, 1996.

Berry, Gordon L., and J.K. Asamen, *Children and Television: Images in a Changing Sociocultural World.* Newbury Park, CA: Sage Publications, 1993.

Bloom, B. *Developing Talent in Young People.* New York: Ballantine, 1985.

Boyd, Charles L., D. Boehi, and R. Rohm. *Different Children Different Needs: The Art of Adjustable Parenting.* Sisters, OR: Multnomah Publishing, 1994.

Boyles, Nancy S. and D. Contadino. *Parenting a Child with Attention Deficit/Hyperactivity Disorder.* Los Angeles, CA: Lowell House, 1996.

Canter, Lee. *Couch Potato Kids: Teaching Kids to Turn Off the TV and Tune in to Fun.* Santa Monica, CA: Lee Canter Effective Parenting Books, 1993.

Case, R. *Intellectual Development: Birth to Adolescence.* New York: Academic Press, 1985.

Cayer, Dibby, T. Harms, and A.R. Ray. *Active Learning for Fives.* Menlo Park, CA: Addison-Wesley, 1996.

—————————. *Active Learning for Fours.* Menlo Park, CA: Addison-Wesley, 1996.

Cline, Foster and J. Fay. *Parenting with Love and Logic: Teaching Children Responsibility.* Colorado Springs, CO: Pinon, 1990.

Coil, Carolyn. *Motivating Underachievers: 172 Strategies for Success.* Beavercreek, OR: Pieces of Learning, 1992.

Cronin, Eileen M. *Helping Your Dyslexic Child: A Guide to Improving Your Child's Reading, Writing, Spelling, Comprehension, and Self-Esteem.* Rocklin, CA: Prima Publishing, 1994.

Curwin, Richard and A. Mendler. *Am I in Trouble? Using Discipline to Teach Young Children Responsibility.* Santa Cruz, CA: E.T.R. Associates, 1990.

Davis, L. and J. Keyser. *Becoming the Parent You Want to Be.* New York: Broadway Books, 1997.

deBono, Edward. *Teach Your Child How to Think.* New York: Penguin, 1992.

DeHaven, Richard W. *How to Guarantee Your Child's Success...and Your Own, Too!* Davis, CA: Mayaland Press, 1994.

Dinkmeyer, Don, G.D. McKay, and J.S. Dinkmeyer. *Parenting Young Children.* Circle Pines, MN: American Guidance Service, 1989.

Dinkmeyer, Don and G.D. McKay. *Raising a Responsible Child: Practical Steps for Successful Family Relationships.* New York: Fireside Books, 1973.

——————————. *The Parent's Handbook: STEP (Systematic Training for Effective Parenting)*. Circle Pines, MN: American Guidance Service, 1989.

Doman, Glenn. *What to Do About Your Brain-Injured Child*. Garden City Park, NY: Avery Publishing Group, 1994.

Draze, Dianne and A. Tornquist. *Creative Problem Solving for Kids*. San Luis Obispo, CA: Dandy Lion Publications, 1994.

Dreikurs, Rudolf. *The Challenge of Child Training*. New York: Hawthorn Books, 1972.

——————————. *The Challenge of Parenthood*. New York: Hawthorn Books, 1958.

——————————. and V. Stoltz. *Children the Challenge*. New York: A Plume Book, 1964.

——————————. and P. Cassel. *Discipline Without Tears: A Reassuring and Practical Guide to Teaching Your Child Positive Behaviors*. New York: A Plume Book. 1972.

——————————. S. Gould and R. Corsini. *Family Council*. Chicago: Henry Regnery Company, 1974.

——————————. and L. Grey. *A New Approach to Discipline: Logical Consequences*. New York: Hawthorn Books, 1968.

Dunn, Opal. *Help Your Child With a Foreign Language: A Parents' Handbook*. London: Hoddler and Stoughton Educational, 1994.

Eagle, Carol and C. Colman. *All That She Can Be: Helping Your Daughter Maintain Her Self-Esteem*. New York: Fireside Books, 1993.

Elium, Jeanne and D. Elium. *Raising a Daughter: Parents and the Awakening of a Healthy Woman*. Berkeley, CA: Celestial Arts, 1994.

Elkind, David. *The Hurried Child: Growing Up Too Fast Too Soon*. Reading, MA: Addison-Wesley Publishing Company, 1988.

——————————. *Miseducation: Preschoolers at Risk*. New York: Alfred A. Knopf, 1987.

Fisher, Gary and R. Cummings. *When Your Child Has LD: A Survival Guide for Parents*. Minneapolis, MN: Free Spirit Publishing, 1995.

Flack, Jerry D. *Talent Education: Strategies for Developing the Talent in Every Learner.* Englewood, CO: Teacher Ideas Press, 1993.

Fraiberg, Selma H. *The Magic Years: Understanding and Handling the Problems of Early Childhood.* New York: Fireside, 1959.

Fuller, Cheri. *How to Grow a Young Music Lover: Helping Your Child Discover and Enjoy the World of Music.* Wheaton, IL: Harold Shaw Publishers, 1994.

Galbraith, Judy. *The Gifted Kids' Survival Guide: For Ages 10 and Under.* Minneapolis, MN: Free Spirit Press, 1984.

Gardner, Howard. *Frames of Mind: The Theory of Multiple Intelligences.* New York: Basic Books, 1983.

——————————. *Multiple Intelligences: The Theory in Practice.* New York: Basic Books, 1993.

——————————. *The Unschooled Mind: How Children Think and How Schools Should Teach.* New York: Basic Books, 1991.

Geralis, Elaine (Ed.). *Children with Cerebral Palsy: A Parents' Guide.* Bethesda, MD: Woodbine House, 1991.

Golant, Mitch and D. Corwin. *The Challenging Child: A Guide for Parents of Exceptionally Strong-Willed Children.* New York: Berkeley Books, 1995.

Gordon, Thomas. *P.E.T. (Parent Effectiveness Training).* New York: Penguin, 1970.

——————————. *P.E.T. In Action.* New York: Bantam Books, 1976.

Grant, G. (Ed.). *On Competence.* San Francisco: Jossey-Bass, 1978.

Green, Gordon W. Jr. *Helping Your Child to Learn Math.* New York: Citadel Press, 1995.

Greenough, Beverly Sills. *Children with Autism: A Parents' Guide.* Bethesda, MD: Woodbine House, 1989.

Greenspan, Stanley. *The Challenging Child: Understanding, Raising, and Enjoying the Five Difficult Types of Children.* New York: Addison-Wesley, 1995.

Guilford, J. P. *The Nature of Human Intelligence.* New York: McGraw-Hill, 1967.

Hallowell, Edward M. and J. J. Ratey. *Driven to Distraction: Recognizing and Coping with Attention Deficit Disorder from Childhood Through Adulthood.* New York: Simon and Schuster, 1994.

Harding, Edith and P. Riley. *The Bilingual Family: A Handbook for Parents.* New York: Cambridge University Press, 1986.

Harrison, Felicity and M. Crow. *Living and Learning with Blind Children: A Guide for Parents and Teachers of Visually Impaired Children.* Toronto: University of Toronto Press, 1993.

Healy, J. *Your Child's Growing Mind: A Parent's Guide to Learning from Birth.* Garden City, NY: Doubleday, 1987.

Holbrook, M. Cay (Ed.). *Children with Visual Impairments: A Parents' Guide.* Bethesda, MD: Woodbine House, 1996.

Holt, John. *How Children Fail (revised ed.).* Reading, MA: Addison Wesley , 1982.

——————————. *How Children Learn.* Reading, MA: Addison Wesley, 1982.

Hopson, Darlene Powell and D. S. Hopson. *Different and Wonderful: Raising Black Children in a Race-Conscious Society.* New York: Fireside Books, 1992.

Ingersoll, Barbara D. and S. Goldstein. *Attention Deficit Disorders and Learning Disabilities: Realities, Myths and Controversial Treatments.* New York: Doubleday, 1993.

Karnofsky, Florence and T. Weiss. *How to Improve Your Child's Language and Thinking Skills.* Parsippany, NJ: Fearon Teacher Aids, 1993.

——————————. *How to Make Your Child a Better Listener.* Parsippany, NJ: Fearon Teacher Aids, 1993.

Kastein, Shulamith, I. Spaulding and B. Scharf. *Raising the Young Blind Child: A Guide for Parents and Educators.* New York: Human Science Press, 1986.

Kavanaugh, Patrick. *Raising Musical Kids.* Ann Arbor, MI: Servant Publications, 1995.

Kaye, Peggy. *Games for Learning: Ten Minutes a Day to Help Your Child Do Well in School—From Kindergarten to Third Grade.* New York: The Noonday Press, 1991.

——————. *Games for Math: Playful Ways to Help Your Child Learn Math—From Kindergarten to Third Grade.* New York: Pantheon Books, 1987.

——————. *Games for Reading: Playful Ways to Help Your Child Read.* New York: Pantheon Books, 1984.

Kennedy, Marge. *50 Ways to Bring Out the Smarts in Your Kid: How to Provide Inspiration and Guidance to Enhance Children's Learning in Every Way.* Princeton, NJ: Peterson's, 1996.

Kersey, Katherine C. *The Art of Sensitive Parenting: The 10 Keys to Raising Confident, Competent, and Responsible Children.* New York: Berkley Books, 1983.

Kraehmer, Steffen T. *Heroes: Embracing Your Role as Your Child's Hero.* Minneapolis, MN: Fairview Press, 1995.

Kurcinka, Mary Sheedy. *Raising Your Spirited Child: A Guide for Parents Whose Child Is More Intense, Sensitive, Perceptive, Persistent, Energetic.* New York: HarperCollins Publishers, 1991.

Lazear, D. G. *Seven Ways of Knowing: Teaching for Multiple Intelligence: Handbook of Techniques for Expanding Intelligence.* Palantine, IL: Skylight Publishers, 1991.

Leman, Kevin. *Bringing Up Kids Without Tearing Them Down.* Nashville, TN: Thomas Nelson Publishers, 1995.

Levine, Mel. *Keeping Ahead in School: A Student's Book About Learning Abilities and Learning Disorders.* Cambridge, MA: Educators Publishing Service, Inc., 1990.

Levy, D. (Ed.). *The Best Parent Is Both Parents: A Guide to Shared Parenting in the 21st Century.* Norfolk, VA: Hampton Roads Publishing Company, 1993.

Lindskoog, John and K. Lindskoog. *How to Grow a Young Reader: A Parent's Guide to Books for Kids.* Wheaton, IL: Harold Shaw Publishers, 1989.

Luvmous, Josette and S. Luvmous. *Natural Learning Rhythms: How and When Children Learn.* Berkeley, CA: Celestial Arts Printing, 1993.

Lynn, George T. *Survival Strategies for Parenting Your ADD Child: Dealing with Obsessions, Compulsions, Depression, Explosive Behavior and Rage.* Grass Valley, CA: Underwood Books, Inc., 1996.

MacDonald, Margaret Read. *The Parent's Guide to Storytelling: How to Make Up New Stories and Retell Old Favorites.* New York: Harper Collins Publishers, 1995.

MacGregor, Cynthia. *Raising a Creative Child: Challenging Activities and Games for Young Minds.* New York: Citadel Press, 1996.

Mackoff, Barbara. *Growing a Girl: Seven Strategies for Raising a Strong, Spirited Daughter.* New York: Dell Publishing, 1996.

Manassis, Katharina. *Keys to Parenting Your Anxious Child.* Hauppauge, NY: Barron's Educational Series, 1996.

Mandel, Harvey, S. Marcus, and L. Dean. *"Could Do Better": Why Children Underachieve and What to Do About It.* New York: John Wiley and Sons, Inc., 1995.

Marone, Nicky. *How to Father a Successful Daughter: Reassuring Advice for Fathers to Help Their Daughters Become Happy, Confident Women.* New York: Fawcett Crest, 1988.

Marsh, Carole. *Math for Girls: The Book With the Number to Get Girls to Love and Excel in Math.* Berkeley, CA: Gallopade Publishing Group, 1989.

McCullough, Bonnie Runyan and S. Monson. *401 Ways to Get Your Kids to Work at Home.* New York: St. Martin's Griffin, 1981.

McNamara, Barry E. and F. J. McNamara. *Keys to Parenting a Child with a Learning Disability.* Hauppauge, NY: Barron's Educational Series, 1995.

——————. *Keys to Parenting a Child with Attention Deficit Disorder.* Hauppauge, NY: Barron's Educational Series, 1993.

Medwid, Daria and Weston, D. C. *Kid-Friendly Parenting With Deaf and Hard of Hearing Children.* Washington, DC: Gaullaudet University Press, 1995.

Micklus, Samuel. *Make Learning Fun: Activities to Develop Creativity.* New York: Creative Publications Inc., 1988.

————————. *Problems to Challenge Creativity.* New York: Creative Publications Inc., 1989.

Mooney, Margaret E. *Reading to, With, and by Children.* Katonah, NY: Richard C. Owen Publishing, Inc., 1990.

Moynihan, Patricia M. and B. Haig. *Whole Parent Whole Child: A Parents' Guide to Raising a Child With a Chronic Illness.* Wayzata, MN: D.C.I. Publishing, Inc., 1989.

Odean, Kathleen. *Great Books for Girls.* New York: Ballantine Books, 1997.

Paquette, Penny and C.G. Turttle. *Parenting a Child with Behavior Problems.* Los Angeles, CA: Lowell House, 1995.

Perkins, Pamela. *Family Literacy: Parents as Partners.* Westminster, CA: Teacher Created Materials, Inc., 1995.

Phillips, Nancy. *Choosing Schools and Child Care Options: Answering Parents' Questions.* Springfield, IL: Charles C. Thomas Publishers, 1994.

Poland, J. *The Demanding Child.* New York: St. Martin's Paperbacks, 1996.

Popkin, Michael. *Active Parenting: Teaching Cooperation, Courage, and Responsibility.* New York: Harper San Francisco, 1987.

Quin, Wilma Rae. *Understanding Childhood Deafness.* San Francisco, CA: Harper Collins Publishers, 1996.

Rathvon, Natalie. *The Unmotivated Child: Helping Your Underachiever Become a Successful Student.* New York: Fireside, 1996.

Rein, R. P. and R. Rein. *How to Develop Your Child's Gifts and Talents During the Elementary Years.* Los Angeles, CA: Lowell House, 1994.

Reisner, Helen (Ed.). *Children with Epilepsy: A Parents' Guide.* Bethesda, MD: Woodbine House, 1988.

Renke, Adria. *Easy Home Tutoring.* Brewster, MA: Stony Brook Publishing, 1995.

Riley, James, M. Eberts and P. Gisler. *Helping Children with Mathematics.* Glenview, IL: Good Year Books, 1996.

Rimm, Sylvia. *Keys to Parenting the Gifted Child.* Hauppauge, NY: Barron's Educational Series, 1994.

Rimm, Sylvia. *Why Bright Kids Get Poor Grades: And What You Can Do About It.* New York: Crown Trade Paperbacks, 1995.

Rynders, John E. and J. M. Horrobin. *Down Syndrome: Birth to Adulthood, Giving Families an Edge.* Denver, CO: Love Publishing Co., 1996.

Sears, William and M. Sears. *The Discipline Book.* New York: Little, Brown and Company, 1995.

Sears, William. *The Fussy Baby: How to Bring Out the Best in Your High-Need Child.* New York: A Signet Book, 1987.

Schulman, Michael and E. Mekler. *Bringing Up a Moral Child: A New Approach for Teaching Your Child to Be Kind, Just, and Responsible.* New York: Doubleday, 1994.

Schultze, Quentin J. *Winning Your Kids Back From the Media.* Downers Grove, IL: Inter Varsity Press, 1994.

Silberg, Jackie. *Games to Play with Babies.* Beltsville, MD: Gryphon House, 1993.

——————. *Games to Play with Toddlers.* Beltsville, MD: Gryphon House, 1993.

——————. *Games to Play With Two-Year-Olds.* Bartsville, MD: Gryphon House, 1994.

Sinic, Marjorie R., M. McClain, and M. Shermis. *The Curious Learner: Help Your Child Develop Academic and Creative Skills.* Bloomington, IN: Grayon Bernard Publishers, 1992.

Slaughter, Judith Pollard. *Beyond Storybooks: Young Children and the Shared Book Experience.* Newark, DE: International Reading Association, 1993.

Smith, Romayne (Ed.). *Children with Mental Retardation: A Parents' Guide.* Bethesda, MD: Woodbine House, 1993.

Smith, Sally L. *Succeeding Against the Odds: How the Learning Disabled Can Realize Their Promise.* New York: J.P. Putnam's Sons, 1991.

Stenmark, Jean Kerr, V. Thompson, and R. Cossey. *Family Math.* Berkeley, CA: Lawrence Hall of Science, 1986.

Sternberg, R.J. *Beyond IQ.* New York: Cambridge University Press, 1985.

——————. and D.K. Detterman (Eds.). *What Is Intelligence?* Norwood, N.J.: Ablex, 1986.

——————. *The Triarchic Mind.* New York: Viking, 1988.

Stoddard, Lynn. *Growing Greatness: Six Amazing Attitudes of Extraordinary Teachers and Parents.* Tucson, AZ: Zephyr Press, 1995.

Stray-Gundersen, Karen (Ed.). *Babies with Down Syndrome: A New Parents' Guide.* Bethesda, MD: Woodbine House, 1995.

Tobias, Cynthia. *Every Child Can Succeed: Making the Most of Your Child's Learning Style.* Colorado Springs, CO: Focus on The Family Publications, 1996.

Trelease, Jim (Ed.). *Hey, Listen to This: Stories to Read Aloud.* New York: Penguin Books, 1992.

Ulene, Art and S. Shelov. *Discovering Play: Loving and Learning with Your Baby.* Berkeley, CA: Ulysses Press, 1994.

Vygotsky, L.S. *Mind in Society: The Development of Higher Psychological Processes.* Cambridge, MA: Harvard University Press, 1978.

Walker, Sally Y. *The Survival Guide for Parents of Gifted Kids: How to Understand, Live with, and Stick Up for Your Gifted Child.* Minneapolis, MN: Free Spirit Publications, Inc., 1991.

Warner, Sally. *Encouraging the Artist in Your Child (Even if You Can't Draw): 101 Failure-Proof, Home-Tested Projects for Kids 2–10.* New York: St. Martin's Press, 1989.

Webb, James T., E. A. Meckstroth, and S. S. Tolan. *Guiding the Gifted Child: A Practical Source for Parents and Teachers.* Dayton, OH: Ohio Psychological Press, 1982.

Weinhouse, Donald and Marilyn Weinhouse. *Little Children, Big Needs: Parents Discuss Raising Children with Exceptional Needs.* Niwot, CO: University Press of Colorado, 1994.

White, Burton. *The New First Three Years of Life.* New York: Fireside Books, 1985.

——————. *Raising a Happy, Unspoiled Child.* New York: Fireside, Books, 1994.

Williams, Wendy M. *The Reluctant Reader: How to Get and Keep Kids Reading.* New York: Warner Books, 1996.

Wood, David. *How Children Think and Learn.* Cambridge, MA: Blackwell Publishers, 1988.

Zuboff, S. *In the Age of the Smart Machine.* New York: Basic Books, 1988.

ABOUT THE AUTHOR

Don Weinhouse, Ph.D. is on leave of absence from his position as a professor of education in the Center for Teaching, Learning, and Research at the University of Southern Colorado and is presently an early childhood adminis-trator at the Taipei American School in Taipei, Taiwan, Republic of China.

Over the past 25 years he has taught in early childhood, elementary, and special education, directed the American School in Japan Nursery-Kindergarten, and served as a professor of early childhood education and early childhood-special education at two other universities.

He is the author of *Little Children, Big Needs: Parents Discuss Raising Children with Exceptional Needs* (1994, University Press of Colorado). Don lives in Taipei, Taiwan with his wife Marilyn and daughter Rachel.